THURROCK TECHNICAL COLLEGE

The Japanese Print since 1900

THE JAPANESE PRINT SINCE 1900
Old dreams and new visions

LAWRENCE SMITH

Published for the Trustees of the British Museum by British Museum Publications Limited

© 1983 The Trustees of the British Museum

Published by British Museum Publications Ltd,
46 Bloomsbury Street, London WC1B 3QQ

British Library Cataloguing in Publication Data

Smith, Lawrence
   The Japanese print since 1900.
   1. Prints, Japanese   2. Prints—20th century
   I. Title
   769.952   NE1323
ISBN 0-7141-1424-3

Designed by Roger Davies
Set in 'Monophoto' Photina
and printed in Great Britain by
Jolly & Barber Limited, Rugby

The Trustees of the British Museum
acknowledge with gratitude the support of
Galerie 39 of London in the publication of
this book.

Page 1
139. Toshiyuki Shiroki (b. 1938). *Dissolve*,
1981. Copperplate, mezzotint

Pages 2–3
42. Hasui Kawase (1883–1957). *Shirahige in
the snow*, 1920. Woodblock

Pages 4–5
102. Reika Iwami (b. 1927). *February water*,
1977. Woodblock

Front cover
30. Shinsui Itō (1898–1972). *Young girl
washing*, 1917. Woodblock

Back cover
96. Jōichi Hoshi (1913–79). *Young tree*,
1975. Woodblock

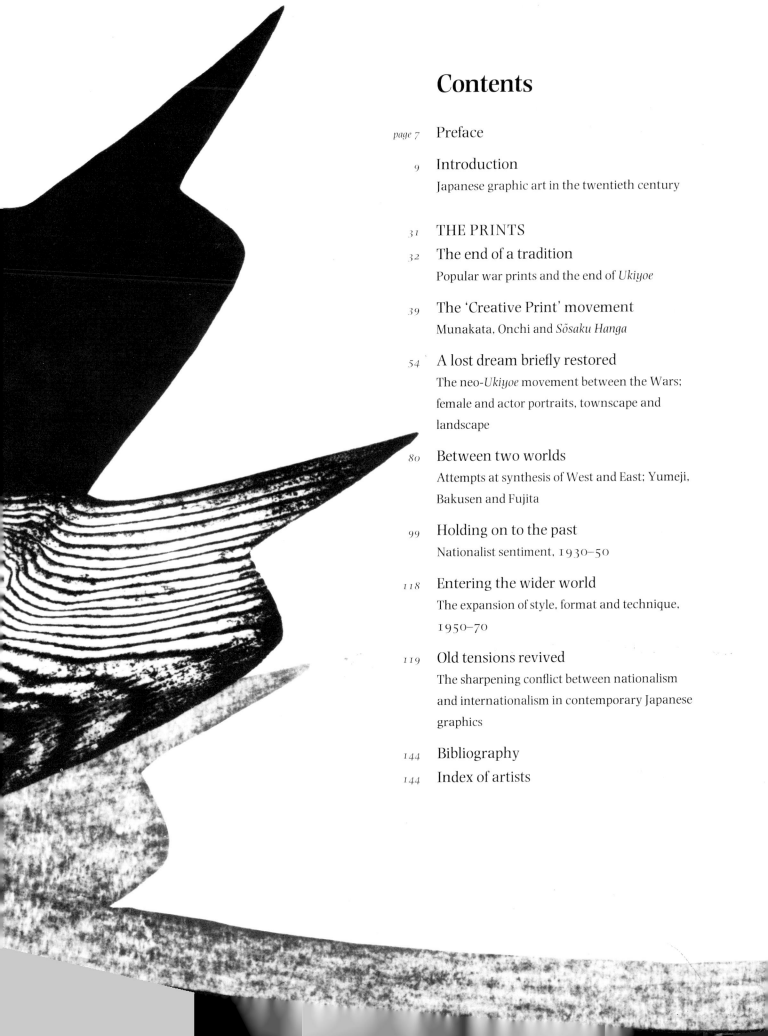

Contents

Preface

The British Museum's collection of Japanese prints and illustrated books of the period up to 1900 is one of the best in the Western world. Until 1980, however, the coverage of the graphic work of the twentieth century had been rather neglected, a neglect which began before 1920 with the very commonly held belief that Japanese prints were no longer worth collecting as they were no longer Japanese. In 1980 the Trustees of the British Museum began the process of filling the gap by setting aside special funds to buy prints of this century. Out of that decision has come the present book, most of the works illustrated in it having been acquired in the last three years.

Special thanks are owing to those who have helped with the book, most of all to Galerie 39 of London who have made it possible to include fifty colour plates. The excellent photographs were taken by David Gowers and his colleagues of the British Museum Photographic Service. Much essential work on the collection and the preparation of the book has been done by Greg Irvine of the Department of Oriental Antiquities, and the whole text was typed by Jennifer Kelly with great patience. Finally, we must acknowledge the many occasions on which Mr Jack Hillier has provided help, information and encouragement during the writing of the book.

21. Shikō Munakata (1903–75).
Shells, from the series 'A Homage to Shōkei', 1945. Woodblock

LAWRENCE SMITH
Keeper of Oriental Antiquities

3. Kōtō. *Picture of the great naval battle outside the port of Lushun* (detail). 1904. Woodblock

Introduction

Japanese graphic art in the twentieth century

The end of a tradition

Popular war prints and the end of *Ukiyoe*

The word *Ukiyoe* will be used often in this book. It is a Japanese term meaning 'Pictures of the Floating World' and refers to a school of art which flourished from the mid-seventeenth century onwards. It holds a pre-eminent place in the history of graphics, for its artists designed the prints which today are still the best-known aspect of Japanese art, and which were themselves deeply influential on the art of the West in the second half of the nineteenth century.

The 'Floating World' was the frivolous urban scene in Japan's great cities – Kyoto, Osaka and Edo. Edo had been renamed Tokyo in 1868 when the Emperor Meiji made it his official residence, and that strengthened even more its position as the centre of popular art. However, that art had already lost the condition which above all made it unique – Japan's seclusion from the rest of the world. The seclusion had began as an official policy in 1639, and ended after years of doubt in 1853 when Commodore Perry of the US Navy sailed into Uraga Bay with his powerful steam-driven 'Black Ships' to negotiate terms for his country.

The prints on sale at that time in Japan were readily available to the foreigners who now began to pour in, finding them enchanting because they were so native and so different. Their subjects were inward-looking – the women of the entertainment districts, the actors of the Kabuki stage, Japanese scenery and townscape. These had been the three great themes since the late eighteenth century; but since the austere Tempō Reform (1841–3) the first two had been discouraged as too frivolous, so it was landscape which held the field in quantity and quality. A new craze for prints of the legendary and historical past arose in the 1830s but did not survive into the twentieth century.

The arrival of the Westerners threw the traditional Japanese print into confusion which was to last until the decade 1890–1900. Standards began to collapse as *Ukiyoe* artists temporarily lost confidence in the value of their style. They found it almost impossible suddenly to absorb European perspective, light and shade, and naturalism into a style which had been based on outline, flat colour and methods of composition unique to East Asia. Before 1890 only Kiyochika (1847–1915) and Yoshitoshi (1839–92) produced a synthesis which was at all successful.

The woodblock medium itself began to be deserted by many publishers for the Western processes of engraving, lithography and wood engraving, all of which could produce larger editions more cheaply, and the arrival of aniline dyes in the 1860s reduced the woodblock print to new depths of garish insensitivity. The low standards of most (though not all) Western visitors, who would buy anything which looked traditional enough, hastened the technical decline.

Subject-matter was very much affected by the influx of Western culture, and one of the last outbursts of the genuine *Ukiyoe* print for Japanese consumption was a result. This was the *Yokahama-e*, a pictorial record of the Americans and Europeans now settling in Yokohama across the bay from Tokyo. These prints

6. Seihō Takeuchi (1864–1942). 'A bird
on a river-pile and a peasant in the rain',
from *Seihō Shūgajō*, 1901. Woodblock

were designed and produced in Tokyo in the old way in the decade 1860–70,
and only their subjects were foreign.

These prints were, however, something almost new in Japanese graphic art –
pictorial journalism of current affairs. During the Seclusion there had been a
few prints done at Nagasaki of the Dutch and Chinese traders allowed there,
and earlier still the fall of Osaka Castle in 1615 had been recorded in the crudest
woodblock-printed broadsheets. However, the repressive Tokugawa govern-
ment had for over two centuries strictly prohibited any comment on political
affairs, and the Seclusion itself eliminated foreign adventures. With the Meiji
Restoration in 1868, it soon became acceptable within reason to depict recent
events. The great Satsuma Rebellion of 1879 was extensively recorded in
sweeping designs marred by aniline dyes.

This new journalistic tendency was to lead to a last, vigorous revival of the
true popular tradition of the woodblock print in the pictorial reports on the
wars abroad on which Japan embarked, beginning with the Sino–Japanese
conflict in 1894–5. That victory established Japan's position as a military
nation, and it gave a new confidence to artists like Gekkō Ogata (1859–1920)
and Hanko Kajita (1870–1917) who knew their prints would be received with
nationalist rapture.

There was a new artistic confidence as well. After a generation European
methods of depicting a crowded scene, with a clearly defined foreground, middle-
ground and far distance all dynamically linked, had been absorbed. The sense
of movement, so necessary to depict scenes of military action, had been learned
from the study of classical European painting. Ways of depicting light and
shade by quietly gradated colour blocks had been integrated with the basic
black outline. It had been found that colours did not need to be violent to be
effective.

These traits can all be seen in Hanko's three-sheet print of Japan's next
foreign escapade, the suppression of the Boxer Uprising in 1900 (no. 1). With
this date we begin our story, for Japan's joining the European powers in the
relief of the foreign community in Peking marked her full acceptance by the
Western world. This psychologically important moment preceded by only four

years the first 'Creative Print' in the French style (see next section).

The Russo–Japanese War of 1904–5, with the dramatic naval victories over the Russian fleet, produced prints of even greater virtuosity and with a sense of violent movement never before so successfully achieved in Japan. The exploding warship *Petropavlovsk* keels over into a sea naturalistically depicted with blocks in grey, green and black, a most convincing transformation of European oil-painting method into graphic form (no. 2). The sea battle off Port Arthur carries across six whole sheets a horrifying confusion of searchlights, explosions, waves and driving snow (no. 3). Yet gone are the stylised waves of Far Eastern tradition. For all this the technical production remains the same as in the past. The blocks are restricted to the size of a cross-section of cherry-wood, carved by a separate craftsman and printed by another based on the artist's sketches.

Back home the favourite *Ukiyoe* subject of elegant fashionable women had also benefited from these trends towards more refined colour and a fuller assimilation of European pictorial method. Shuntei, for example, contrasted the stronger tones of the foreground figure with very pale ones in the background scene – an obvious enough trick to a Westerner, but something new and exciting to the Japanese (no. 4). This delicate style, however, expressing in part the West's fantasies about picturesque Japan, led nowhere, and by the end of the Meiji era in 1911 popular *Ukiyoe* had finally died. The small, ultra-refined prints of birds, flowers, animals and insects by Koson Ohara (1877–1945), often on a pale grey background, were perhaps the last gasp. Immensely popular in the West, they are still found there in large numbers, having clearly been exported in some bulk.

Outside the popular tradition some prints were still made in the period 1900–10 continuing an alternative ideal which had flourished for two centuries in Kyoto, Osaka and Nagoya. Mainly in book and album format, they attempted to reproduce in graphic form the flavour of an artist's original painting, rather than popular work designed for prints. Such are the book after Seihō (no. 6) and the album after Sekka (no. 7), both printed in Kyoto. These higher aspirations of the print were soon to be taken over and transformed by the 'Creative Print' movement.

The 'Creative Print' movement
Munakata, Onchi and *Sōsaku Hanga*

The term *Sōsaku Hanga* means 'Creative Prints' and came into general use among artists and critics after the formation of the *Nihon Sōsaku Hanga Kyōkai* – 'The Japanese Creative Print Society' – in Tokyo in 1918. Its ideals were to dominate one side of Japanese graphics up to the Pacific War. From 1945 until about 1970 *Sōsaku Hanga* became virtually the graphic establishment of Japan. Since then its direct influence has declined, but its central tenet, that an artist should take part in every process in the production of his prints, has come to be almost universally accepted in Japan.

Great artists are never typical of anything; Onchi and Munakata are chosen as the major figures for discussion because of their achievement rather than their influence. Onchi (1891–1955) did take part in most of the group activities of the *Sōsaku Hanga* artists and was regarded as their moral leader for thirty years, yet he was very unorthodox in almost every aspect of his art. Munakata (1903–75) never associated formally with the movement at all, but he fulfilled

11

9 *left*. Takeji Fujishima (1867–1943).
*Two scenes in the rain, c.*1905. Woodblock

13 *above right*. Takashi Itō (1894–).
Sunset: Inside the moat of Tokyo University,
1923. Woodblock

its ideals of raising the print to the level of high art even more thoroughly than Onchi and became a legend inside and outside Japan in the last twenty years of his life.

What they had in common was devotion to the idea of the print as a primary, creative work of art which was not a reproduction of something else. Talented Japanese artists had been visiting Europe, usually France, since 1884 when the painter Seiki Kuroda (1866–1924) went there. He was gradually followed by more and more, who became aware that in France an original artist could be as well-known for prints as for paintings, or that his reputation might even, like Toulouse Lautrec's, be based on prints. That such artists might cut their own blocks, engrave their own plates, or prepare their own surfaces for lithography, and then take their own impressions was an even greater difference, though it had long been a commonplace in Europe. Such independence from the commercial pressures of publishers must have seemed enviable, as well as the influence over quality which only a very well-established artist in Japan could hope to have over the block-cutters and printers.

Even artists who had not visited France were by 1900 becoming very aware of Western graphic styles through art journals, limited exhibitions, and most of all through themselves working as illustrators in newspapers, magazines and books. In most cases this sort of work was more up-to-date than that for sheet prints. Kanae Yamamoto (1882–1946), the man regarded as the founder of *Sōsaku Hanga*, was himself trained as a wood engraver. In this process lines are cut *into* small blocks, not left in relief as in the traditional Japanese method, and the resulting print consists mainly of ink or colour with white lines or patches showing against it. The emphasis is thus thrown on to the ink pigment rather than the line.

This move away from line is an important characteristic of the *Sōsaku Hanga* style, and it already existed among Western-style painters like Fujishima (1867–1943) who probably did not produce their own prints. His two scenes in the rain, very reminiscent of illustrations, are of this type of 'white on black' style

12. Hanjirō Sakamoto (1882–1969).
*Street corner meeting at the town hall,
Kōchi,* from the series 'Thirty Views of
Tosa', *c.*1925. Woodblock

(no. 9). It reappears in Itō's *Sunset* twenty years later (no. 13), a work printed
and published by the very commercial Watanabe (see next section).

Yamamoto's belief was that the old woodblock medium should be united
with artistic involvement in all the processes and with Western style, and in
1904 he produced the first of his very rare sheet prints in this manner. Obviously
only small editions could be made, and none of the early artists can have earned
much money from their work. Instead, they began to publish small prints in
their own magazines, like *Hōsun* (1907) and *Tsukubae* (1914).

Among *Hōsun*'s founders was Hakutei Ishii (1882–1958), and its early
contributors included Hanjirō Sakamoto (1882–1969) and Kazuma Oda
(1882–1956). These young painters in the Western style, all born in the same
year, show the real diversity of attitude within early *Sōsaku Hanga*. Hakutei in
his 'Twelve Views of Tokyo' (no. 5) designed images of a traditionally *Ukiyoe*
type, in which only the small inset landscapes have a relaxedly French atmosphere. He was one of several *Hōsun* artists who employed the artisan Bonkotsu
to cut their blocks, apparently abandoning one of the main tenets of the group –
but in fact keeping to its spirit by retaining artistic control.

Sakamoto's views of town and country (nos 11–12) are of the three the
closest in technique and style to mainstream *Sōsaku Hanga* work before the
Pacific War. They are very French in flavour, although they depict Japanese
scenes. He cut his blocks himself in a deliberately unpolished way, leaving the
grain and the marks of the cutting tools very visible. Colours are applied thinly,
giving a surface half-way between a water-colour and a lithograph. The palette
is of pastels and greys. Where outline is used, it is thick, soft and fractured. This
style, strangely enough, was brought to Japan first by the painter Kunzō Minami
(1881–1951) who studied in England between 1907 and 1910, but his very
rare prints nevertheless have that overwhelming Frenchness which dominated
western Europe at the time.

Oda actually did lithographs, contrary to the usual practice of the group,
inspired by the great French lithographers such as Toulouse Lautrec, Bonnard

and Vuillard. By 1924, however, he had began to design woodblocks for the very commercial publisher Watanabe, who represented in one sense everything the group was trying to get away from. It is difficult to claim, though, that his work loses by it. In *The Great Bridge at Matsue* (no. 70) Watanabe's cutters and printers reproduced with great sensitivity a snowy scene which had a soft, flowing quality clearly related to the artist's lithographic style. By the next year, in *Mihonoseki in Izumo* (no. 71), the technique is closer to woodblock, but the quiet casualness of the scene is very French in atmosphere. It is significant that Oda was the only *Sōsaku Hanga* artist to appear in the Toledo Exhibition of 1930, which was overwhelmingly of works published by Watanabe and Yoshida, and that no reference is made in the catalogue to the new group; only his exceptionally 'European' quality is mentioned.

In the last analysis it is this European preference which marks out most *Sōsaku Hanga* artists rather than any aesthetic or technical ideals, and their leader Kōshirō Onchi certainly thought of himself as part of an international scene. The son of a tutor to the Imperial family, he was educated in the highest possible Japanese circles; but although he never lost his aristocratic confidence and refinement of perception, he was always in practice a rebel and an innovator, both in art and in poetry. One of the founders in 1914 of the magazine *Shirakaba*, he became in the 1920s the acknowledged leader of *Sōsaku Hanga*.

Nevertheless, even he was deflected by the lack of general acceptance of his work and by the growing nationalism and repression of his nation into representational Japanese subjects (nos 16–18) which in the end he did not favour so much as abstraction. After contributing, it seems from a sense of solidarity, to some nostalgic books and portfolios just after the War (nos 88, 90), he worked more and more on the pure abstracts which had been his first love since as early as 1914 and which now found complete favour in a Japan firmly allied to the Western democracies (nos 14–15).

To Onchi, according to his pupil Sekino, it was the actual printing which was the moment of excitement. He thought of each print as an individual work of art, and indeed he differed from most of his colleagues in doing very little painting and drawing at all. As a result his editions are very small (sometimes one only). *May Landscape* (no. 14) consisted of only ten prints. Fortunately for the rest of the world he did contribute to portfolios and illustrated books, and allowed some of his most famous images to be printed by trusted colleagues (nos 15, 19). In the study of Japanese art what 'rules' exist are immediately broken!

Shikō Munakata achieved even greater independence through a combination of luck and personality. One of fifteen children of a poor family from the north, he decided at an early age to become the 'Van Gogh of Japan'. From the mid-1930s he began to pour out his vigorous, almost manic prints, always full of natural movement. Although obviously influenced by his early studies of Western art, especially Matisse, his real driving forces were Zen Buddhism and Japanese folk tradition. Both can be seen in his great pre-war *Rakan* series (no. 20) and in his *Shōkei* series (no. 21), his first after the War which destroyed most of his blocks. These politically uncontroversial tendencies gave him independence from public opinion before and after the War, when he gradually became Japan's most famous print artist since Hiroshige (d. 1858).

To Munakata cutting the blocks was the central act of artistic creation, and he rarely kept to his sketches. Rather the blocks *became* his sketches, and he kept them to take infrequent impressions from throughout his life. They were, too, a version of ink painting to him, and he normally printed only in ink. Colours were added by hand, in many cases to the back of the print so that they glowed through the thin paper. As with Onchi, each print had become as individual as a painting. The ideals of *Sōsaku Hanga* had reached their zenith.

A lost dream briefly restored
The neo-*Ukiyoe* movement between the Wars; female and actor portraits, townscape and landscape

If true popular *Ukiyoe* died around 1910, it did not take long to come alive again in a new form. This phenomenon, which lasted as an artistic force to be reckoned with for only twenty-five years, was called *Shin Hanga* – 'New Prints'. It was the old Japan's answer to *Sōsaku Hanga*, and the two of them made the period 1915–40 one of the most interesting and productive in the history of the Japanese print.

The man behind this movement was the publisher Shōsaburō Watanabe, who became as important in developing and encouraging artists as his famous predecessor Tsutaya Jūsaburō in the late eighteenth century. His part in the process is best explained in his own words from his catalogue of 1951 (at which time he had twice revived his business after partial destruction – once after the earthquake of 1923, again after the bombs of 1945):

In 1907 . . . we started producing medium and small-sized new colour prints for foreign connoisseurs. . . . Flattering ourselves that from this experience we had been able to grasp some of the spirit of the best old masters, we proceeded to study how really good modern colour prints could be created, with the help of several painters who were especially appreciative of our project. In this way in 1915 we produced *Woman in the Bathroom* by Goyō Hashiguchi, in 1916 *Looking into the Mirror*, an ambitious attempt by Shinsui Itō, then a young painter of unusual talent, and in 1918 and after landscape prints by Hasui Kawase.

In picking on these artists to design for prints Watanabe showed good instincts, for all three were to rank among the major figures of the *Shin Hanga* movement. Hasui and Shinsui remained the great artistic assets of his company until their deaths in 1957 and 1972 respectively. It is significant, though, that Goyō soon turned to publishing his own works, as did Hiroshi Yoshida (1876–1950), whom Watanabe interested in prints around 1920.

All four of these artists proved highly successful in commercial terms, and it is clear that his feeling for what his public would buy was one of Watanabe's great assets. Why, then, did two of his major discoveries stay with him while two did not? The answer seems to be that Goyō and Yoshida, for all their differences of temperament, were both basically trained in Western methods, and could not give up the independence which was implied in that training. Both, too, were older and better-established men. Shinsui and Hasui both received their most important training from the *Ukiyoe* painter Kiyokata Kaburagi (1878–1973), who strangely outlived both of them. Kiyokata did little graphic work, and what he did was charming rather than remarkable, but he must have been an inspiring teacher within the more traditional system, and it was no accident that his pupils were at their best designing prints for an authoritarian publisher. Other pupils of Kiyokata were Shūhō Yamakawa (1898–44, no. 44), Shirō Kasamatsu (1898–, nos 77–80, 82) and Kotondo Torii (1900–77, no. 45). Kotondo, from a very old artistic line, used several publishers.

It is clear from Watanabe's own statement that his business in its earliest years depended more on well-informed foreign buyers. It continued to do so into the 1930s. He and Yoshida had dominated the big exhibition of *Shin Hanga* in Toledo in 1930 and the one there almost as big in 1936, but deteriorating relations with the democratic Western nations from then on turned his efforts back to Japan. Fortunately for him and his artists he had made his big internal breakthrough with his first major exhibition in Tokyo in 1932.

This Western market had a good and a bad side. The European and American taste for the traditional subjects, formats and styles of *Ukiyoe* did help to encourage another generation of artists who might otherwise have done little graphic work. Watanabe realised that the recent European tradition of the limited edition could be used to raise standards and at the same time ensure the edition would be sold, and at a good price. In the eighteenth century fine prints had been limited by quality alone. Watanabe revived those standards of excellence but added the proof of exclusivity by numbering his editions. Westerners, and soon Japanese buyers themselves, were encouraged by this into seeing themselves as buyers of discernment. *Ukiyoe* had moved in ten years from the popular to the exclusive.

The dangers of this Western-dominated market were that such prints would either perpetuate a touristy Japaneseness of subject and style or else become nearly indistinguishable from Western representational art. Both, in fact, did happen – the first in the sometimes over-sweet Japanese beauties of Kotondo (no. 45) or the later Shinsui (no. 38), which are just redeemed by their superlative design and printing; the second in the picturesque but shallow landscapes of Yoshida (no. 81) and the later Hasui (no. 73). This side of *Shin Hanga* survived the War, degenerating quickly into tourist art.

This, the worst side of *Shin Hanga*, was more than balanced by its achievements, which drew genuine inspiration from the past of *Ukiyoe* and from the present example and practice of Western art. Curiously enough, it was the young Shinsui and Hasui, later embodying many of the more negative tendencies, who guided by a still receptive Watanabe did some of the most outstanding prints of the period 1915–25. First, however, we must consider the older artist who first succeeded in this synthesis, Goyō Hashiguchi.

Goyō had been trained as a Western-style painter. Like many of his fellows, he made a living as an illustrator for books and magazines. Although he worked in woodblock, it was in a racier, more relaxed style than that of traditional *Ukiyoe*. He was the first major artist to be asked by Watanabe to design a print, and its success led him to reassess the *Ukiyoe* style of depicting women and to see how it could be brought to life again. He saw clearly that at its best it combined strong but refined design with attention to detail. It was his insistence on a super-perfection of printing, including *gauffrage* and the application of powdered mica, which led him to publish his own prints from 1918 until his early death in 1921, and which accounts for the smallness of his output. In fact, most of his major prints of beauties were done in the year 1920 (nos 24–9).

Goyō did more than simply return to an old ideal. His mastery of human posture was learnt from the West, relying not only on the textiles and hairstyles, as in the past, but also on the body, and his woman seen from the back (no. 26) is the first successful nude in the Japanese print. He also added an enigmatic quality which had been missing from *Ukiyoe* women since the early nineteenth century and was now restored through the example of the French

32 above. Shinsui Itō (1898–1972). *Early summer bath*, from the series 'Twelve forms of new beauty', 1922. Woodblock

50 above right. Shunsen Natori (1886–1960). *Portrait of the actor Kōshirō Matsumoto in the part of Ikyū*, 1929. Woodblock

intimiste artists. His prints of beautiful women have a mixture of mystery, sensuality and elegance which recall the work of Utamaro (1753–1806), to whom all the *Shin Hanga* artists looked as a model. Goyō, rather than Shinsui or Yumeji (see next section) deserved the often-awarded title of 'the new Utamaro'.

To this situation the young Shinsui added ardour. In his early prints of women there is a youthful passion as well as a simplicity and clarity of expression which made him the perfect instrument for Watanabe's 'New Prints'. His *Young girl washing* (no. 30) has a fresh, youthful eroticism never seen before in the sophisticated world of *Ukiyoe*. Emotional force way beyond his nineteen years can be felt in *Sudden shower* (no. 31), and this, too, is achieved with a simplicity which is truly graphic. He continued to design masterpieces in this vein up to the great earthquake of 1923 (nos 32–3). Thereafter his prints became less passionate, always beautifully designed and produced but with a slickness that approaches the reproductive (nos 34–8). In fact, Shinsui's fame as a very polished painter of screens and hanging scrolls in the *Ukiyoe* style grew during the decade 1920–30, and after 1930 many of his prints are reworked from paintings (nos 35, 38). After 1945 his part in the process of reproduction became minimal.

43. Hasui Kawase (1883–1957). *Rain at Uchisange, Okayama*, from the series 'Selected Landscapes', 1923. Woodblock

Utamaro was the great model for prints of women. A more recent artist, Andō Hiroshige (1797–1858), had dominated the popular landscape prints and had found no successor. The important influence of European landscape painting and graphics since the 1880s had had an outlet in *Sōsaku Hanga*. Again Watanabe inspired the young Shinsui to revive the traditional landscape. Their 'Eight Views of Lake Omi' (1917–19) showed artists that it was possible to combine French and Japanese pictorial construction, to widen the range of expression to include darkness, storm and cloud, to use Western stylisations of cloud and water (no. 41b), and yet to include all these in the traditional small format, using ink outline filled in with colour blocks.

Shinsui did little good landscape after this. His method was taken up by Hasui Kawase (1883–1957) with great success (nos 42–3). Like Shinsui, he did his most sensitive work up to the time of the earthquake, after which it became increasingly glib as he turned to full-time designing for endless series of landscapes. Others, however, were to find new vitality in the landscape and townscape print (see p. 23).

Hasui's over-production and slickness after 1923 seems to have been in rivalry with Hiroshi Yoshida, already a well-established painter of mountain landscapes by 1920. Yoshida's technical contribution was to find a method of reproducing in woodblock the rich, colourful effect produced in his oil-painting by adjacent patches of colour. He did this by using an unusually large palette of pigments for printing, and to separate patches by a quiet, grey line which merged into the darker colours (no. 81). Thus he managed to prevent his tones from smudging into each other when taking the impression, without the obtrusive, clear black line of traditional prints. This extremely 'scenic' technique was adopted by Hasui (nos 73–4), but neither he nor Yoshida can be said to have improved on their landscapes of the early 1920s.

The 'New Prints', like old *Ukiyoe*, had a third favourite subject in the actors of the Kabuki theatre, and this was a field where the Japanese connoisseur and theatre-goer must have been more important than the foreign collector. Again it was Watanabe who encouraged artists to design for prints which would recapture the glories of the actor portraits of Sharaku (working 1794–5) and who identified a suitable young talent in Shunsen Natori (1886–1960, nos 49–53). This genre needed least alteration from the examples of the past and shows the least influence of the West. The extravagance of its subjects seemed to suit the period 1920–30, but it began to decline rapidly with the approaching shadows, leaving a small but distinguished body of prints to crown an honourable tradition. The dreams of *Shin Hanga* of a restoration of beautiful, colourful prints glorifying Japan's picturesque traditional culture were to fade with astonishing speed.

Between two worlds
Attempts at synthesis of West and East; Yumeji, Bakusen and Fujita

The period between the two World Wars was one of strong polarisation into artistic camps. As we have seen, in the field of the print this division was expressed in the markedly different ideals of *Sōsaku Hanga* and *Shin Hanga*. In painting the difference was even more accentuated between *Yōga* ('Western painting') and *Nihonga* ('Japanese painting'), both of which were very well established in the 1920s. These artistic trends reflected profound internal differences about social and political policy and Japan's place in the world.

58. Gesson Okamoto (1876–1931). 'Deck listening', from *Gesson Gashū*, 1934. Line block

Some artists and publishers fell into neither camp, reflecting instead the complexities of the cultural scene in their many permutations. *Sōsaku Hanga* at this period leaned towards Western themes in European style (atmospheric landscape and townscape, lower class life in towns, still life); and *Shin Hanga* favoured more native preoccupations (women in traditional dress, the Kabuki theatre, famous tourist spots) in a Japanese style. Others, however, reflected a much more fluid world, depicting Western subjects in Japanese style, traditional subjects in European style, or evolving a mixture taken from any of these elements. Some, too, depicted the Tokyo world where these conflicting trends took physical shape in the fashions and lifestyle of the rich and the Bohemian (no. 64).

The central figure is Yumeji Takehisa (1884–1934), celebrated as a painter in a thoroughly vigorous, individual and mixed style. The original prints made under his supervision in the years 1914–16 are very rare, but something of their simple, direct flavour can be seen in his dinner menu design for a Japanese passenger ship in 1929 (no. 65).

In itself this thoroughly French menu with its surrounding design of a girl dressed for one of Japan's most traditional festivals symbolises the two worlds across which Yumeji stretched his lively talent. Her face, too, has a slight edge of satire in it which comes from the European tradition. It has none of the inscrutability and calm of Shinsui's rather similar subject (no. 36).

There is a subtle transference of European facial expression in the faces of Yumeji's women, from those in the most modern, Western dress and make-up (no. 64) to those in whose manners there is no apparent hint of outside influence. The lady dressing her hair in *Frog*, for example, could be 100 years earlier, except for the undeniably 'twenties' cast of her face. Yumeji's ability to convey the urban flavour of his age made him very popular among the more sophisticated and led to technically excellent prints being made after his paint-

N. Y. K. LINE

MENU

HORS-D'ŒUVRE
MARY WIDOW CRAB COCKTAIL
RIPE OLIVES   HEART OF CELERY   MIXED NUTS
VELOUTE OF RAFRAICHE
DELICE MAHIMAHI FLORIDA
SUPREME BREAST OF CAPON CLAMART
CAULIFLOWER HOLLANDAISE
MIGNONETTE POTATOES
RACING KING SALAD
ROYALE SOUFFLE PUDDING SAUCE SABAYON
(ICE CREAM) OLGA PLAZA   FRIANDAISES
CORBEILLE DE FRUITS
DEMI TASSE
M. S. "ASAMA MARU"
Tuesday, October 22, 1929

65. Yumeji Takehisa (1884–1934). *The Tanabata Festival*, a design for the dinner menu of the M.S. *Asama Maru*, 1929. Woodblock

ings and drawings during and after his lifetime (nos 63a–b, 64). In themselves these prints represent a further conflict, for they are on the one hand reproductive and on the other genuine and successful attempts to convey the flavour of a most individual artist.

One of the publishers of Yumeji's works, Katō, did prints also of Tsuguji Fujita (1886–1968) who literally moved between France and Japan, spending long periods in each, before finally taking French citizenship in 1955 where he was known as Leonard Foujita. His outstanding etched self-portrait (no. 60), c.1922, is completely Western in technique and style, as were most of his

68. Hiroaki Takahashi (1871–1944).
Belled cat, *c*.1935. Woodblock

paintings. Yet Katō published a print of one of them which uncannily fuses the two worlds (no. 61). It is in a standard Japanese format, in the traditional woodblock technique, but it is undeniably close to Fujita's refined oil-painting style, and of course the woman is actually Western. Her expression, though, is oblique, and she does not look at us, as Yumeji's very confident and Westernised seductress does (no. 64). In that respect Katō's print of Fujita's *Akita Girl* (no. 62) is not so different from his blonde lady in evening dress. However, the nationalist sentiment leading Fujita to portray a simple peasant of northern Honshū was tearing him apart. He stayed in Japan and supported his country throughout the War, only returning to France and much criticism in 1949.

An equally complex fusion can be felt in the work of Toraji Ishikawa (1875–1964), notably in a set of prints he designed specially for the woodblock medium in 1934 (nos 66–7). They show fashionable women in various activities. One is set in a completely traditional bath-house. Her plump face and figure, lips made up in a pout, and short, boyish hair reflect the Western fashions of the time. Another shows a similar woman in a notably untraditional posture and situation, naked on a large red mat, accompanied by a sleeping cat; but she is looking at a book of prints in the style of Utamaro.

Nowhere are the contradictions of the period more marked than in the rare prints of Bakusen Tsuchida (1887–1936). He was one of the best painters in the *Nihonga* style, that movement which represented pure Japanese spirit and technique in painting. Yet he was an expert draftsman in the European manner, and when he came to publish his book *Bakusen Gashū* (1921) he chose a large Western format, with collotype reproductions of his paintings, interspersed with little woodblock vignettes in the European manner for what was a manifesto of the *Nihonga* style. The paper, however, was of superb, Japanese hand-made quality, watermarked with his name in Chinese characters, and he inserted in the book a group of woodblock recreations (no. 57) of his sketches of *maiko* (Kyoto dancing girls). These prints straddle the world of the European sketch and the world of the reproductive Japanese print.

The landscapes of Oda have been mentioned (see p. 15), similarly mixed in subject and atmosphere. Other artists, like Konen (1878–1940), designed townscapes and landscapes which seemed uncertain of their emotional direction. Often such prints have great charm and a sense of time and place; but the times were changing, and Japan was now moving in a direction which was far from ambiguous.

Holding on to the past
Nationalist sentiment, 1930–1950

The great earthquake of 1923 had shaken Japan's sense of security after thirty years of steady political and material advance. The Great Depression of 1929 led to greater pessimism and hardship, and a realisation that Japan was still at the mercy of a world dominated by the Western colonial and industrial powers. The easy, comparatively liberal atmosphere of the Taishō era (1911–24) rapidly vanished, and by 1931 the country was on the road to totalitarianism and war. With this came suspicion of the rest of the world. Artists who practised foreign styles were less popular, especially the *Sōsaku Hanga* printmakers with their rather left-wing political heritage, though it would be inaccurate to say they were repressed.

This situation existed up to 1945. Artistic styles which were thoroughly Japanese in subject and flavour naturally thrived – *Nihonga* in painting, the products of the recently formed Folk Art movement in the crafts. From the latter came a revival of the old print medium of stencil, as seen in the books and albums of Keisuke Serizawa (b. 1895), though his *Don Kihōte* of 1936 was made at the request of a European on a European theme (no. 59). Its style, however, is antiquely Japanese. Munakata, too, benefited from an atmosphere receptive to his Buddhist subject-matter, which excluded all but the world of Asia, expressed in his individual, semi-mystical, but recognisably Japanese style.

Naturally the *Shin Hanga* prints gained in favour as well from the turning inwards of Japanese sentiment. On the whole the results were not good, and the prints of women began to suffer from a stolid nationalism; it was more important that they should be Japanese than that they should be interesting. In landscape, too, there was a tendency towards a rather glib glorification of the Japanese scene; during the decade 1930–40 the output of Yoshida and Hasui was very large, and their over-assured technique made depth of feeling unnecessary for their success (nos 73, 81).

Nevertheless, the inwardness of the period, its apprehension and uncertainty, did produce some prints of real feeling and charm among lesser figures. All of them seemed at their best in small-scale scenes of towns, villages or buildings where the positive values of traditional Japan and its ordinary people were not inflated by the grandiose. Even Hasui was sometimes affected by this mood (no. 74). It is not surprising in the rather apprehensive atmosphere leading to the Pacific War that the prints are often most effective depicting scenes in snow, rain, mist or darkness. Ironically, the ability to represent darkness convincingly came only in the late nineteenth century, and was learned from Europe.

Among these artists three stand out in the 1930s as definite but minor talents – Kōitsu Ishiwata (b. 1897), Shirō Kasamatsu (b. 1898) and Tōshi Yoshida (b. 1911). All reflect the uncertainty and worry underlying the

79 *above.* Shirō Kasamatsu (1898–).
*Spring Snow – the Shimakoshi Shrine at
Asakusa*, 1934. Woodblock

89 *above right.* Jun'ichiro Sekino (1914–).
An Oiran's street procession, from the
portfolio 'Native Customs in Japan', 1946.
Woodblock

nationalist surge; their figures are small and retiring, often with their backs
to the viewer. Kōitsu's love for the domestic detail of Japanese small-town and
village life preserved him from the inflation of his teacher Hasui (nos 75–6).
Shirō's melancholy sense of nocturnal atmosphere produced some haunting
images (nos 77–80, 82) which stay just on the right side of the sentimental.
Tōshi, son of Hiroshi Yoshida, in his powerful series of small prints 'Tokyo at
Night' (1938), approached, uniquely among *Shin Hanga* artists, a sense of
black desolation among familiar scenes (nos 83–6). None of these artists did as
good work after the War.

The eclipse of *Shin Hanga* in the years immediately after the War is simple to
explain. They were replaced in favour of the *Sōsaku Hanga* artists who now
finally came into their own. Men like Maekawa, Hiratsuka, Sekino, Kawanishi
and Onchi were appreciated by many of the Americans serving now with the
occupation forces. They were not tainted with old-fashioned nationalism; their
history of political liberality and outward-looking internationalism made them
suddenly popular in all quarters. More importantly, perhaps, their tradition of
strong-minded independence and personal creativity allowed them to survive
the disasters of the War spiritually unscathed.

Through this strange turn of events Onchi and his group became the new
artistic establishment in the Japanese print, and they took on them the task of
helping repair Japan's shattered image and self-respect through an art which
would show the positive, creative, peaceful side of national culture. Thus the

internationalists became nationalists in their turn. In 1946 some of the members of the Japanese Print Association co-operated on three portfolios of small, modest prints called respectively 'Native Customs in Japan', 'Scenes of Last Tokyo', and 'Woman's Customs in Japan'. All the contributors cut their own blocks, but the actual printing was done by Takamizawa. The national sentiment of these prints is quieter and far subtler than in the past, and also far wider. Kawakami's view of a lurid Ginza (no. 87) could now safely incorporate the pseudo-European world of Tokyo in the 1920s, a marked contrast to Shirō's romantic Ginza (no. 82). Onchi's *geisha* has a world-weary, slightly bitter sophistication (no. 88b), and his pupil Sekino is able to treat with derision an *Oiran*'s procession, one of the great idealised subjects of *Ukiyoe* in the past (no. 89).

Entering the wider world
The expansion of style, format and technique, 1950–70

Just as two generations before, prints lagged behind painting and sculpture. By 1950 Western-style painting in Japan had almost caught up with developments in Europe and the USA. Artists were able to express freely the residual horrors of the holocaust in often violent surrealist or abstracted images.

In prints, however, developments were slow in style and technique. The period 1950–70 became the age of the consolidation and flowering of *Sōsaku Hanga*, which now went into a third phase of great confidence. Until the American withdrawal in early 1952 many of the artists seemed to retain the need to hang on to Japan's past, and their work has an introverted quietness which is easily recognisable. Thereafter they grew in confidence and also began to grow apart, losing their sense of cohesion and becoming more individual.

They also began to be internationally known and to realise that they could actually make a living as full-time printmakers through worldwide sales. Munakata led the way, winning first prize at the São Paulo *biennale* in 1955 and embarking in his last twenty years on a period as Japan's most famous

93. Kiyoshi Saitō (1907–). *Winter in Aizu*, c.1965. Woodblock

94. Gaku Onogi (1924–76). *Landscape (afterimage)*, *c*.1968. Silk-screen

artist, though it must be said that he never sought fame. The American collector Oliver Statler contributed much to the fame of the *Sōsaku Hanga* artists through his book *Modern Japanese Prints – An Art Reborn* (Preface dated 1956), where he introduced to the Western public twenty-four of them, plus the descendants of Hiroshi Yoshida whom he evidently felt able to include, in spite of their *Shin Hanga* roots, because they published their own prints. It is interesting to see how established many of these artists already were. Of the thirteen who contributed to the 1946 portfolios ten were described by Statler, including Onchi who had only recently died. Looking through Statler's pages now, one is struck, with the exception of Munakata, by how quiet these artists are; and with the exception of Onchi, how little abstraction had obtruded. Saitō with his muted, semi-abstracted views of Japanese country life was to prove one of the most popular in the West.

Three of them – Hiratsuka, Maekawa and Azechi (no. 91a) reappeared in James Michener's *The Modern Japanese Print: An Appreciation* (1962), a work which marked the high-water mark of old-style *Sōsaku Hanga*. Michener, an enthusiast for contemporary prints, organised with the publisher Tuttle a competition to choose ten artists to be included in his book, which was to be published in an edition of 510, each volume including a set of the prints. The judges were all Westerners – some in New York and some in Tokyo – and their final choice was again a triumph for the *Sōsaku Hanga* establishment. There was little that was difficult or challenging in the winning prints, with the exception of Sadao Watanabe's *Listening*, which can claim to be his finest work (no. 91b). There was, however, a move towards gently abstract compositions among the younger winners (Reika Iwami, Masaji Yoshida and Tomio Kinoshita), which provided some much-needed new vigour.

Iwami herself (nos 102–3), Tōkō Shinoda (nos 100–1) and Onchi's pupil Rikio Takahashi (nos 98–9) have since then worked this vein with single-minded elegance. They were among the first, with Saitō, to enlarge the format of their prints to the much more generous dimensions which have since become usual. Such prints are no longer for portfolios. They are for the walls of modern houses, galleries, and most of all for the great print *biennale* shows in the world's cities.

Meanwhile, the modern Western world was rapidly entering the consciousness of younger printmakers. Some of them had since around 1950 begun to explore the centuries-old European intaglio methods of engraving, etching, aquatint, mezzotint and wood-engraving. Among them was Chimei Hamada, the first Japanese printmaker since Fujita to produce masterpieces in a foreign style and idiom (no. 112). His work is a decisive break with the now old-fashioned world of *Sōsaku Hanga*. In the 1960s the enigmatic Gaku Onogi seized on the silk-screen medium to translate into prints his extraordinary blue visions already expressed in his oil-paintings.

The decade 1960–70 saw a decisive shift of consciousness among younger artists away from the old artistic leaning to Europe. It was replaced by the USA, where a number of them now began to live and work for substantial periods. Some, like Ay-Ō, participated in the Pop Art revolution (no. 131); some, like Miyashita, absorbed recent and contemporary ideals into an elegant synthesis (nos 128–30); others, like Matsubara, worked in the USA with little impact on her traditionalist prints except in subject-matter (no. 113).

Old tensions revived
The sharpening conflict between nationalism and internationalism in contemporary Japanese graphics

Since 1970 Japanese prints have become part of the international world of art. Many artists exhibit at the world's *biennales* and regularly do well. Japan's old tradition of immaculate craftsmanship and sense of design has not been lost, and ensures that their works almost always compel notice. At the same time the Japanese public has become fully aware of the print to collect or to put on a wall in a frame. The development of the international-style apartment in Japan's great cities has produced a décor in which prints like those of Kazumasa Nagai (no. 132) find a natural place.

The move to internationalism extends not only to subject-matter but also to technique. Until 1975 about 50 per cent of professional print artists were still working in the ancient woodblock medium of the Far East. That is no longer true, although woodblock remains important, and younger artists like Morozumi (nos 124–5) and Shigeyuki Kawachi (nos 126–7) have found new resources of expression within it, while Jōichi Hoshi in the last astonishing years of his life raised skill in cutting blocks to greater heights than ever before (nos 95–7). Now, however, more printmakers are exploring with fresh inspiration the old European intaglio technique (nos 138, 139) and using with as much enthusiasm as other international artists the contemporary media of silk-screen, often using photographic images (nos 136–7). In style the tendency towards the

106 *above.* Sadao Watanabe (1913–).
Feet washing, 1972. Stencil

112 *above right.* Chimei Hamada (1917–).
Eroding Town A, 1977. Engraving,
aquatint

109 *opposite.* Mitsuhiro Unnō (1939–).
Kinasa in light snow, 1974. Woodblock

abstract, inherent in Japanese calligraphy, ink painting and in the native *Rimpa* school of printing and design, has finally achieved a position of full acceptance as a normal and fruitful means of expression.

Opposed to these trends there remain many printmakers of a decidedly traditional outlook, who normally use woodblock, and landscape and townscape remain their favourite themes, as in the work of Mitsuhiro Unnō (no. 109) and Fumio Kitaoka (no. 108). Their prints seem to be the inheritors of the late aspirations of *Shin Hanga* but using the *Sōsaku Hanga* method. An even more national design style can be seen in the prints of Yoshiharu Kimura (no. 110). At present the artists of pure native sentiment seem to lack conviction and vigour. They also lack an outstanding figure in the younger generation.

The international artists have just such a figure in Tetsuya Noda (nos 114–23), whose work has continued to enthral connoisseurs throughout the world since the late 1960s. Noda uses his own photographs as the basis for his prints, which only achieve their full impact when seen in reality. Then their weighty seriousness can work through their surprisingly large size. Because his photographs record deeply felt moments in his life, they have the direct humanity of a major artist's sensitivity. By converting them into big silk-screen images, enhanced with pale areas of woodblock pigment, he makes them more universal and less direct. They have the intensity, inwardness and obliqueness of much traditional Japanese art; they also have the direct humanity which it has often lacked. Noda has through his prints shown that today the ancient conflict between Japaneseness and non-Japaneseness can be resolved.

1974.5. みつひろ

141. Mokuden Fujimoto
(1895–). 'Studies of bamboo',
from *A Picture Album of the
Four Noble Plants*, 1973.
Photographic reproduction

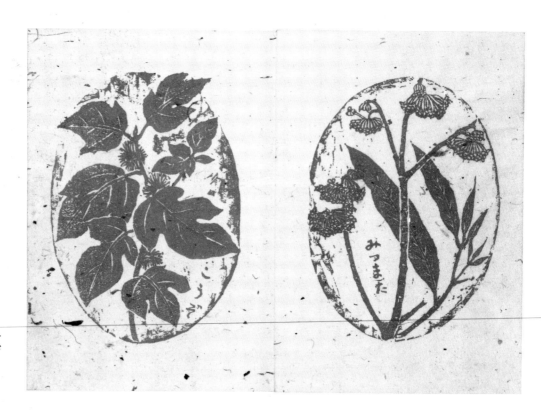

142. Rokurō Mutō (1907–).
'The Paper Mulberry and the
Mitsumata Plant', from *Tie-
dyeing and woodblock*, 1978.
Woodblock

143. Tsunemitsu Konishi
(1940–). 'Rainwater basin'
(left) and 'Mountain entrance
of the Jōjakkōji', from *One
Hundred Views of Sagano*,
1975. Photographic repro-
duction from pen and ink
drawing

The end of a tradition

NOTE: In the catalogue of illustrations and wherever an artist's name is quoted in full, the family name is given second, and the art-name or personal name first. This is the usual practice for artists of the twentieth century, although it is a matter of personal preference or sometimes simply chance which of the two names has come to be popularly used. On the whole, the artists who have worked in the *Ukiyoe* or neo-*Ukiyoe* styles are known by art-names (for example, Shinsui), while the *Sōsaku Hanga*, Westernising and contemporary artists tend to use the family name (for example, Onchi, Fujita, Noda).

The sizes given normally refer to the whole sheet. Exceptions are mentioned individually.

Titles are translated into English where the original is in Japanese. Many titles of more recent prints are in English only, or in both languages, in which case the English is quoted.

The publisher and printer are given. Where they are not mentioned, it may be assumed that the artist published and printed himself, as is nearly always the case with *Sōsaku Hanga* artists.

Previous page
29. Goyō Hashiguchi (1880–1921).
Combing the hair, 1920. Woodblock

1 Hanko Kajita 1870–1917

The Japanese at the gates of Peking
1900
Woodblock in three sheets,
each 375 × 256mm
Printed and published by Heikichi Matsuki,
Tokyo
1946.2.9.090. Bequeathed by
Arthur Morrison. Illustrated page 34

As the twentieth century opened, the old journalistic aspect of the Japanese print had received new life from the country's growing policy of foreign involvement. In 1894–5 the war with China had stimulated many prints in the vivid but traditional three-sheet format, some of which had been designed by Kajita as an official war artist. In 1900 he again turned his hand to depicting the Japanese intervention in the Boxer Rebellion, which Japan and the Western powers united to suppress. The full title is translated: 'The Allied Armies attack on Peking. Picture of the Japanese Army taking the Chaoyang Men' (one of the gates). Kajita was trained in the painting style of the Maruyama–Shijō school, which can be detected in his fondness for mist and cloud and for delicate colours, in spite of the violence of the subject. The strong sense of recession, learned from Europe, is balanced by the almost formalised clouds of smoke linking the three sheets of the picture, a carry-over from the ancient device of linking screen and handscroll compositions by clouds and mist.

2 Kōkyo

The destruction of the Petropavlovsk
From the series 'Latest pictorial news of the Russo–Japanese War'
June, 1904
Woodblock, 289 × 434mm
Printed and published by Heikichi Matsuki,
Tokyo
1907.5.22.7. Illustrated page 33

The Russo–Japanese war of 1904–5 saw the culmination of the journalistic print, the main events being relayed to the Japanese public in vigorously graphic form by official artists, some of whom were on the spot, and reaching them often in less than two months. This print, designed 'By request', shows the defeat of a Russian squadron under Admiral Makharov. The descriptive cartouche translates: 'The battleship *Petropavlovsk* while engaged with our Third Squadron was surprised by the sudden appearance of our First Squadron, and while escaping to port hit a mine. More than 700 officers and men under Makharov died.' The artist is not recorded, but the fact that the first element of his name is the last element of Gekkō's suggests that he was the latter's pupil. He is *not* the Kyoto painter Taniguchi Kōkyō (1864–1915), who was the first teacher of Seifu Tsuda (no. 10).

2

7

33

1

3 Kōtō

Picture of the great naval battle outside the port of Lushun
May, 1904
Woodblock, in six sheets,
each 370 × 240mm
Published by Hōkichi Kimura, Tokyo
1906.12.20.1681. Illustrated page 8

This *tour de force* of multi-sheet print design, by a little-known pupil of Gekkō Ogata (1859–1920), records the Japanese defeat of the Russian fleet early in the Russo–Japanese war. Lushun, in Manchuria, leased to the Russians at the time, was known to the British as Port Arthur. Part only of this expansive composition is illustrated. It combines descriptive movement with a characteristically Japanese patterning of searchlights slicing through the snowy black night, surging waves and exploding shells. It is surprising to note that this print had reached the British Museum by December, 1906; it formed part of Arthur Morrison's collection, which was bought by the Museum.

4 Shuntei Miyagawa

worked *c*.1887–1907
Mimeguri
From the series 'A pictorial mirror of famous places in Tokyo'
1903
Woodblock, 378 × 265mm
Published by Heikichi Matsuki, Tokyo
1906.12.20.1652. Illustrated page 35

During the period 1890–1910 printed female portraits returned to the mood of refinement and exoticism of a century earlier, although this was achieved at the cost of personality and mystery. Shuntei was one of the artists who began tentatively to inject those missing elements, and who thus laid the way for the *Ukiyoe* revival of Goyō and Shinsui (nos 24–40). In this print he combines traditional detail with a very low point of view which shows the powerful influence of recent French art. The woman is hanging up *obi* (sashes) and kimonos to air. Across the pond is the gateway of a Shintō shrine.

5 Hakutei Ishii 1882–1958

'Asakusa'
From the series 'Tōkyō Jūnikei' ('Twelve views of Tokyo')
1910–16
Woodblock, 378 × 260mm
Published by the artist, but cut by the artisan Bonkotsu Igami
1983.3.12.03. Illustrated page 38

Hakutei, best known as a Western-style painter, was one of the founders of the *Sōsaku Hanga* movement: yet this print series harks back to much older *Ukiyoe* traditions, in subject-matter, construction and technical method. The artist deliberately sought to revive the glories of the past by designing a set of *mitate*, or 'comparisons'. Each district of Tokyo is represented by a beautiful woman who is associated with the small inset view, which is in each case heavily influenced by French style. In this print the view is Kinryūzan, the Buddhist temple at the heart of this Bohemian district of Tokyo, and its associated Shintō shrine; and the young woman is tying braded cords on the *kotsuzumi* (small drums) which are used in Shintō festivals as well as in traditional dance and drama forms. Hakutei was not able at this time to cut his own blocks and commissioned them from a professional artisan of the old type who had been associated with the early days of the *Sōsaku Hanga* movement.

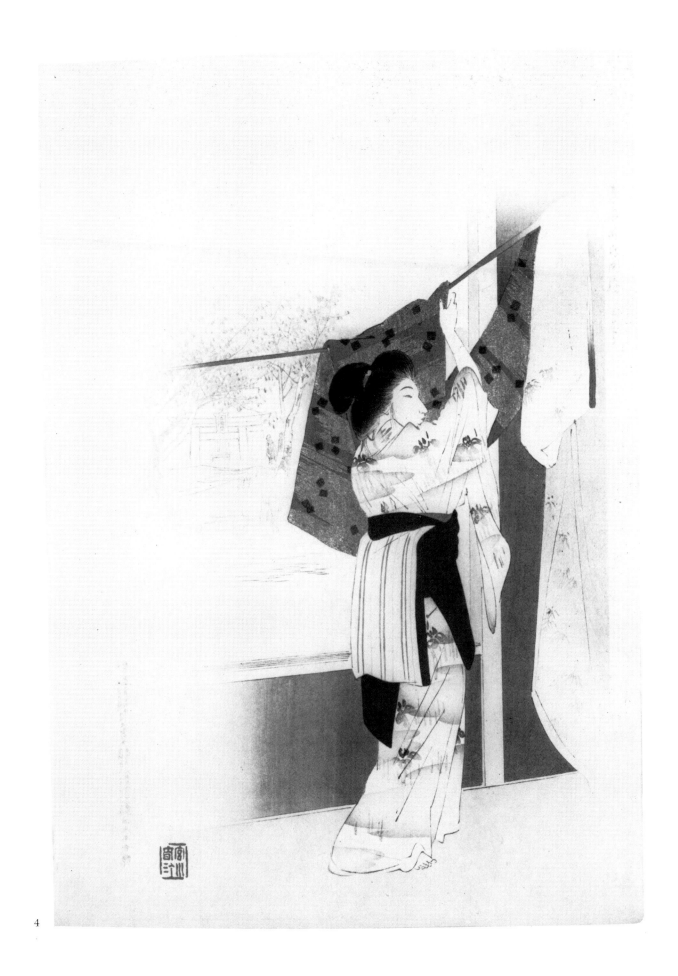

87

22

5

8

6 Seihō Takeuchi 1864–1942

'A bird on a river-pile and a peasant in the rain'
From *Seihō Shūgajō* ('Seihō's Practice Painting Album')
Vol. 1, 1901
Woodblock, each volume 175 × 247mm
Published and printed by Naozō Yamada in association with Murakami Shōbei, Kyoto
1981.8.5.01. Illustrated page 10

Seihō was the last major artist of the Maruyama–Shijō school; following his first visit to Europe in 1900 he created a lively synthesis of Western and Japanese styles. These volumes, however, stand at the end of a tradition over a century old of *gafu*, or 'picture albums', consisting of woodblock reproductions of a specific artist's work and styles. Two of the volumes are in black ink outline, and two are in colour. The black and white designs take advantage of the translucency of Japanese paper so that they show through invitingly before they are reached. Here we see the bird on the left-hand sheet, while we see on the right the peasant in reverse, showing through from the previous page.

7 Sekka Kamizaka 1866–1942

The iris bridges
From the set of albums 'Pictures of a hundred hundred worlds'
1909
Woodblock, 300 × 445mm
Published by Naozō Yamada of the Geisōdō, Kyoto
1980.2.25.01. Illustrated page 33

This *de-luxe* album, which uses gold, silver and mica to aid its effects, is one of several reproducing with great vividness the work of Sekka, who worked for most of his life in a style based on the decorative art of Ogata Kōrin (1658–1716) and his successors. As a graphic work it harks back to the great woodblock book *Kōrin Gafu* of 1803. This little-known masterpiece shows that the Kyoto cutters and printers had lost none of their ability to rise to a commission which required the highest standards of taste and sensitivity. The subject is the *kakitsubata*, a reference to the plank bridges across a pond of purple irises mentioned in the tenth-century poetic classic *Ise Monogatari* ('The Tales of Ise') and much illustrated in all subsequent periods in Japanese art. The iris blooms have been impressed to make them stand out against the green stalks and the mica representing water.

10

The 'Creative Print' movement

8 Takeji Fujishima 1867–1943

The stand at the races
c.1905
Woodblock, 267 × 198mm (sheet)
1906.12.20.1851. Illustrated page 38

Fujishima went to Europe in 1905, and this print, clearly done for publication in a portfolio, is from about that time, though it is not clear whether it precedes the visit. The fact that it is of a Japanese subject suggests that it does. In any case it had entered the collection of Arthur Morrison by 1906 (see no. 3). The races had been a fashionably Western activity in Japan since the early Meiji period, and this scene is almost a mirror-image of the Japonisme then so strong in Western Europe. The notice at top left reads 'All telegrams accepted here'. The printing is in pale monochrome purple only, a particularly European feature.

9 Takeji Fujishima

Two scenes in the rain
c.1905
Woodblock, 267 × 198mm (sheet)
1906.12.20.1846/7. Illustrated page 12

This sheet is probably from the same portfolio as no. 8 and was acquired in the same way. Both show a French-influenced style which had existed since the 1890s in book and magazine illustrations, and which precedes the sometimes very similar work of the *Sōsaku Hanga* artists of the next decade. The most noticeable innovations here are the thick 'frames' to the pictures, the light, washy application of the pigment, and the use of blocks of colour or ink, rather than thin outline filled with colour, to build the composition. In these two prints a light brown is the only colour used. Although Fujishima did little graphic work and is best known as an oil-painter, he was an important figure in transmitting Western ideas to the Japanese artistic world.

10 Seifu Tsuda 1880–1978

Peasants on a cart
From the series 'Small Art Illustrations'
1913
Woodblock, 236 × 399mm (sheet)
Published by Naozō Yamada, Kyoto
1980.1.18.035. Illustrated page 39

This composition is printed in bright red, yellow, blue, brown and white on a beige paper. The artist was in France from 1907 until 1911 and studied under Jean-Paul Laurens, and his portfolio published in Kyoto shows his very strong leanings towards French art. Like many of the pioneer artists who began to take the Japanese print out of its traditional mould very early in the century, he was mainly a Western-style painter and quite naturally saw prints as a concurrent, though less important product. The date of 1904 given to this series by Siegfried Wichmann in *Japonisme* (Thames and Hudson, 1981) seems too early.

88b

11

11 Hanjirō Sakamoto 1882–1969

Harimaya-chō in Kōchi at night
From the series 'Thirty Views of Tosa'
*c.*1925
Woodblock, 260 × 375mm
1968.2.12.09. Illustrated page 42

Like Fujishima, Sakamoto is comparatively
little known as a print artist but has a very
high reputation in Japan as a painter in oils.
However, he was one of the artists active in
the first magazine of the *Sōsaku Hanga*
movement called *Hōsun*, and contributed to
the pioneer set of series 'Print Scenes of
Japan' (1916–20). At this time his landscape
work achieved a most striking abstraction.
During and after his stay in France in
1921–4 Sakamoto produced a number of
landscape and townscape prints combining
French techniques and Japanese sentiment

with a new elegance and vividness. This
series depicts townscapes and landscapes in
and around Kōchi in the south of the island
of Shikoku. The old name of this area was
Tosa. The lightly applied colours are printed
with a grainy 'open' texture which seems
deliberately to recall lithography. The sudden
increase in urbanised life which began in
Japan about 1915 coincided with the influx
of French artistic conventions long developed
to express city scenes, and Sakamoto's
townscapes are as lively as any of the period.

12 Hanjirō Sakamoto

*Street corner meeting at the town hall,
Kōchi*
From the series 'Thirty Views of Tosa'
*c.*1925
Woodblock, 255 × 375mm
1968.2.12.011. Illustrated page 14

The humour of this scene reflects the liberal
atmosphere of the 1920s, which only major
artists like Sakamoto could afford to continue
into the intense and less tolerant 30s.

13 Takashi Itō 1894–

*Sunset: Inside the moat of
Tokyo University*
1923
Woodblock, 266 × 395mm
Published by Shōsaburō Watanabe, Tokyo
1954.11.13.032. Given by Mrs M. B. Happer.
Illustrated page 13

This print is an example of 'Japanised
Japonisme' where the visual structure of the
French prints of the early twentieth century
has in turn inspired a new generation of
Japanese artists. This can be seen specially in
the use of the 'white on black' technique
which, though originally derived from the
stone-rubbing style of the Far East, had
assumed new importance in European
graphics. The most notable users of this effect
were Felix Vallotton and Aubrey Beardsley,
but the German Emil Orlik, who was a
collector of Japanese prints and visited Japan
several times, was a more direct link. This
example is printed in brown, but there is also
a version in black.

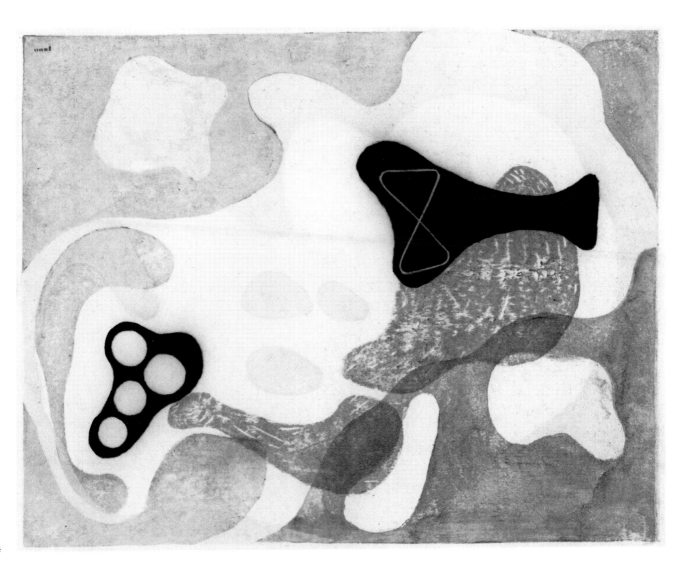

14

14 Kōshirō Onchi 1891–1955

Poème no. 7: May Landscape
1948. 5th of an edition of 10
Woodblock, 407 × 507 mm
1983.3.12.01. Illustrated page 43

This print is also known as *Abstract Poem 7*.
It is a typical work of the last years of Onchi's
life, when in the free artistic climate of the
American occupation and after he felt able
to concentrate on abstract compositions, to
which he had always been temperamentally
drawn. In them he was able to explore in a
very subtle way the relationships between
colours, which he printed over each other in
varying combinations. In this case the colours
are black, grey, yellow and white, and the
design seems to incorporate elements from
the plan of a Japanese rock garden, though
this is not hinted at in the title. Both these
traits are much followed by Onchi's pupil
Takahashi (nos 98 and 99). The print includes
the figure of eight or hourglass motif which
Onchi returned to so many times in his later
works.

15 Kōshirō Onchi

Poème no. 8: Butterfly Season
1948. This example reprinted 1955
Woodblock, 451 × 359 mm
Published by Kōichi Hirai, Tokyo
1982.10.7.07. Illustrated page 37

The print is also known as *Poem no. 8–1:
Butterfly*. This famous image has a confusing
printing history, since a number of reprints
were made after the artist's death as a
memorial edition by Kōichi Hirai, while
Onchi himself did only ten. (See also no. 19.)
This example has Hirai's original slip dated
July, 1955. The title refers to a poem Onchi
wrote at the time which describes a butterfly
emerging from its chrysalis, symbolised by its
enclosed left-hand wing in the print, and
reaching for the sky, symbolised by its free
right-hand wing and the blue clouds.

16 Kōshirō Onchi

Woman after the bath
c.1930
Woodblock, 283 × 254 mm
1982.10.7.08. Illustrated page 46

The style of this untitled print is closest to
Onchi's series of four 'Beauties of the Four
Seasons' (1927–30), a period when he
favoured hot, contrasting pigments
reminiscent of the European Impressionists
he much admired. In this image he has
recreated in a completely individual way the
traditional *Ukiyoe* image of the Japanese
woman, bare to the waist, at her toilet
(contrast Shinsui's neo-*Ukiyoe* versions in
nos 30 and 39 and Goyō's in no. 26).

38

16

18

17 Kōshirō Onchi

View of Tokyo
*c.*1930
Woodblock, 221 × 315mm
1981.7.30.03. Illustrated page 47

The artist has in this memorable print summed up the grim, pessimistic atmosphere of Tokyo after the 1923 earthquake. Gone is the charm of Bohemian urban life, to be replaced by brutalised industrialism; the square, functional shapes stretch apparently endlessly to the blocked-off horizon, and the mood is darkened by the dirty greys and yellows which dominate the palette. This is Onchi's counterbalance to the nostalgia of the series 'A hundred new views of Tokyo' (1928–32) to which he contributed.

18 Kōshirō Onchi

Young woman on a verandah
*c.*1930
Woodblock, 250 × 242mm
1981.7.30.04. Illustrated page 46

The mood and technique of this melancholy print are similar to the artist's *Mirror* (1930) and *Eight aspects of modern women* (1929). In all of these Onchi shows an interest in the back view of women, a device brought to maturity in the prints of Utamaro (1753–1806). The sense of wistful longing brought out by the blank white hillside is a reflection of the disillusioned mood of many artists after the great earthquake of 1923. It is the more poignant for being expressed by a very young woman in festival finery.

19 Kōshirō Onchi

Portrait of the poet Sakutarō Hagiwara
1943. This example from a reprinted edition of 1949
Woodblock, 525 × 420mm
1981.12.14.01. Illustrated page 50

In this, one of his most famous prints, Onchi portrays with tragic intensity his friend Hagiwara (1886–1942). Onchi typically produced only seven inpressions, but this example is from the edition of fifty made in 1949 by Junichirō Sekino, the artist's younger associate (see no. 89). A still later edition was made by Kōichi Hirai (see no. 15). Hagiwara was a leading exponent of nihilistic verse, who much influenced Onchi's own very fine poetry. An alternative title is *The author of the Ice Island*, a reference to one of Hagiwara's major works.

17

20 Shikō Munakata 1903–1975

The rakan *Subodai*
From the series 'The Ten Great Disciples of
the Buddha'
Block carved 1939
Woodblock, 1,023 × 396mm
1981.3.31.02. Illustrated page 51

It is not known exactly how many pulls of
this set the artist took during his lifetime, but
this one was taken after January 1962, when
Munakata was given the honorary Buddhist
title *Hōgan.* The title appears in his seal,
bottom left.

Munakata's primary inspiration in his
pre-war years was the Buddhist folk-tradition
of Japan. In this grand set of ten very large
prints he copied the long narrow format of
the mock hanging-scroll in which Japanese
popular Buddhist prints of the sixteenth and

seventeeth centuries were produced, and also
their use of simple contrasts of black and
white. This example is squared off, as if
bursting out of the confines of the block for
which Munakata had such reverence. The
format in addition made the prints, together
with two extra ones of other deities, suitable
for mounting in facing pairs on a pair of six-
fold screens. The disciple (*rakan*) Subodai is
shown as a Japanese Buddhist monk, but his
exaggerated features and long ears are
traditional in the depiction of the Buddha's
disciples as native Indians.

21 Shikō Munakata

Shells
From the series 'A Homage to Shōkei'
1945. This copy dated 1956 by the artist
Woodblock, hand-coloured, 550 × 390mm
1980.12.27.01. Illustrated pages 6, 54

In this, his first major work after the
War, Munakata paid tribute in a series of
twenty-four prints to the folk-art potter
Kanjirō Kawai and his kiln in Kyoto called
Shōkei. The artist had been a prominent
member of the *Mingei* (Folk Art) movement
since 1936 when he met Kawai. This print,
like all of the series, is both mysterious and
monumental, and its relevance to pottery
uncertain, for the figure is Buddhist in origin.
The peasant-like woman/deity seems both to
be breaking out of the confines of the block
and holding it together. Vivid colours are
applied by hand from the front. The late date
is explained by the artist's habit of not
signing and dating his prints until selling
them.

26

46

19

22 Shikō Munakata

Rainfall
From the series 'Twelve Months:
The Sound of Tea'
1956
Woodblock. 485 × 567mm
1980.12.27.82. Illustrated page 36

One of Munakata's most original techniques
is used here. The black is printed with a
single block. The colours are then applied
from behind by hand on to the thin paper so
that they show through with a strangely
intense glow, in this example in purple, blue,
red, orange and green. Each print thus
becomes unique, and is in fact half-way
between printing and painting. As in many
of the artist's works, the meaning of the
series title is not entirely apparent, although
it is clear that he is referring to the Tea
Ceremony and its origins in Zen Buddhist
meditation. However, there is no way of
avoiding the power and clarity of this
mountain and waterscape in the high
rainy season.

23 Shikō Munakata

Kanaya
From the series 'Munakata's print works of
the Tōkaidō'
1963–4
Woodblock. 630 × 480mm
1981.7.30.012. Illustrated page 54

This technique is similar to no. 22, but
colours are also applied from in front. Ever
since the great series of views along the
Tōkaidō Road by Hiroshige (1797–1858),
painters and print artists in Japan had sought
to do new and original versions of the same
series of fifty-five; but Munakata improved
the number to sixty-two when commissioned
to produce a set by the Suruga Bank. He
did another set still in 1966. The cone of
Mount Fuji on the horizon is reduced to a
starkly geometrical shape which would have
astonished Hiroshige.

20

21

23

A lost dream briefly restored

24 Goyō Hashiguchi 1880–1921

Woman in loose summer kimono
1920
Woodblock, 452 × 296mm
1981.4.10.02. Illustrated page 55

Goyō was devoted to the study of the prints of Kitagawa Utamaro (1753–1806), and it would be fair to claim that he came closest to that blend of adoration, mystification and detachment which characterised the old master's attitude to women. This composition has more than a passing resemblance to some of Utamaro's beauties in semi-*déshabillé*. Goyō's great prints, which are not numerous, were all published by himself between 1918 and his early death in 1921, using the full range of techniques available to the woodblock medium through artisans in the traditional industry.

25 Goyō Hashiguchi

Girl at a hot spring resort
1920
Woodblock, 459 × 301mm
1980.12.27.06. Illustrated page 41

Published in October, this print shows a seasonal reference to reddening maple leaves. Since Goyō published his own prints, he was able to make subtle points of this sort to his own satisfaction. The gesture of holding the towel up to the face was much favoured by Utamaro (see no. 24), but the elegant, yet full-blooded colour contrasts of rust, blue and black give a piquancy which is all Goyō's. The only apparent concession to Western taste is the ring on the finger, but the wistful expression is unmistakably of the late Taishō period.

26 Goyō Hashiguchi

Woman after the bath
1920
Woodblock, 442 × 296mm
1982.10.07.013. Illustrated page 48

The nude body had never been a feature of the art of East Asia, and even the erotic prints of Utamaro had made their effects more by concealment than revelation. Goyō, however, had received a Western-style art education and was much more confident in depicting the female form, though he chose as by traditional instinct a partial back view. This print may be assessed as one of the first thoroughly successful nudes in Japanese art. The lady's left leg, nevertheless, is tucked under her right in the natural posture of a person used to sitting on the floor.

27 Goyō Hashiguchi

Young woman on a verandah
1920
Woodblock, 447 × 267mm
1980.12.27.015. Illustrated page 61

Like the majority of the artist's best prints,
this example was published in 1920. It is full
of the sadness and melancholy characteristic
of his mature work. Issued in July, it shows a
pensive young woman in a summer *yukata*
(cotton bath-robe) decorated with indigo
tie-dyed leaf motifs. The brightly lit colours
and the luscious, summery flowers and
bamboo moving in the evening breeze only
emphasise the cool tones and restrained
mood of the main subject.

28 Goyō Hashiguchi

Woman preparing her sash
1920
Woodblock, 563 × 307mm
1981.4.10.03. Illustrated page 60

This dignified print is one of the last great
female portraits in the *Ukiyoe* tradition, where
the emotion is expressed primarily through
textiles. The lady, dressed in her finest
summer kimono, is preparing her enormously
long and sumptuous silver-brocaded sash
(*obi*), which is represented by mica dust in
the print. On the green *tatami* (mats) lies the
pad which is tied under the *obi* and sustains
its great tucked bow at the back. As usual in
Goyō's late prints, the lady's expression is
mysteriously thoughtful.

29 Goyō Hashiguchi

Combing the hair
1920
Woodblock, 445 × 345mm
1930.9.10.01. Illustrated pages 31, 55

Here Goyō returned to another of Utamaro's
favourite female themes, the combing out of
the long black hair which was normally only
visible to members of the woman's immediate
family, as hairstyles at this period were
always worn up (see no. 26), usually in three
piled buns. The artist was sufficiently confident
in the visual and emotional power of the
girl's loose hair to dispense with the more
subtle technical effects of his later prints, and
has contented himself with a simple blue
yukata (bath-robe) against a silvery ground of
powdered mica.

24

29

大白天七月三半深水
比江人象の物
大人橋

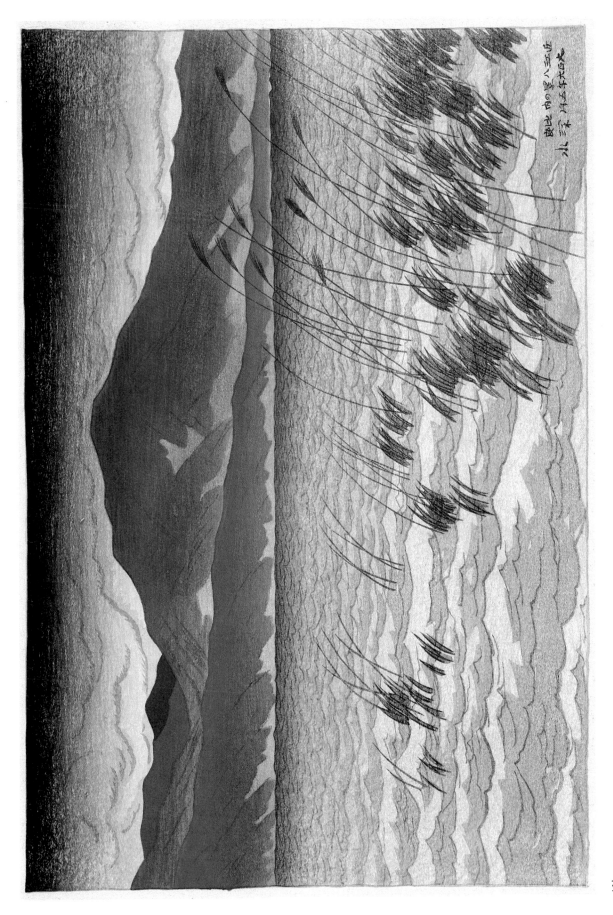

33

34

30 Shinsui Itō 1898–1972

Young girl washing
1917. From a limited edition
Woodblock, 437 × 295 mm
Published by Shōsaburō Watanabe, Tokyo
1946.2.9.082. Illustrated page 66 and front
cover

This is one of Shinsui's earliest masterpieces
done in collaboration with Watanabe, who
may be said to have turned the young *Ukiyoe*
painter in the direction of sheet prints. The
subject of a young girl wringing out her
towel after washing is full of youthful
innocence and ardour, but the composition is
remarkably sophisticated for an artist not yet
nineteen. In it he shows not only his debt to
his teacher Kiyokata but also to the Western
print artists of the previous generation whose
style had been changed by studying the sense
of design of Utamaro and his contemporaries.

31 Shinsui Itō

Sudden shower
1917. From a limited edition
Woodblock, 441 × 305 mm
Published by Shōsaburō Watanabe, Tokyo
1981.8.1.03. Illustrated page 45

This print has an ambiguous power and
emotional maturity rather rare in the artist's
work, and it is all the more remarkable that
it was designed when he was just turned
nineteen years old. Shinsui thought of
himself mainly as a painter in the traditional
formats of the hanging scroll and the folding
screen. Later in his life most of his prints
were in fact closely based on finished
paintings, but in his first years with Watanabe
he seems to have made designs intended only
as prints. Such works often have a gritty,
forceful quality lacking in his rather over-
sweet paintings, and this print is a notable
example of that tendency.

28

28

28

27

32 Shinsui Itō

Early summer bath
From the series 'Twelve forms of new beauty'
1922. From a limited edition of 200
Woodblock, 436 × 266mm
Published by Shōsaburō Watanabe, Tokyo
1946.2.9.083. Bequeathed by Arthur
Morrison. Illustrated page 18

In this set published in 1922 and 1923
Watanabe carried on the old *Ukiyoe* idea of a
continuing series which came out at intervals.
In Shinsui he had a natural talent for a series
of beautiful women. Of all of them this sheet
has the most Westernised image, and the
influence of Renoir and Degas can be seen in
the soft, full figure. Shinsui gives her, however,
a subtly exaggerated definition by the use of
an indented white line. This separates her
from the steam of the bath-house, which is
rather ingeniously represented by the
whorling marks left by the impression of the
baren (a pad used by the printer to press the
paper on to the block).

33 Shinsui Itō

Snowy night
From the series 'Twelve forms of new beauty'
1923. From a limited edition of 200
Woodblock, 434 × 258mm
Published by Shōsaburō Watanabe, Tokyo
1982.10.7.09. Illustrated page 58

This magnificently sombre and suggestive
print is the masterpiece of the series (see
no. 32). Among the blacks and greys a single
tiny corner of scarlet fabric shows where the
woman's hand holds the umbrella.

34 Shinsui Itō

Bath-robe
From the first series 'A Collection of
Today's Beauties'
1929. From a limited edition of 200
Woodblock, 430 × 280mm
Published by Shōsaburō Watanabe, Tokyo
1981.4.10.01. Illustrated page 58

Shinsui was above all a great artist in the
Japanese erotic style, and in the 1920s, a
period of rare free-and-easiness, he designed
a number of fine prints of partly dressed
women. As often in this old tradition, he
achieved the maximum effect from the blue
and white cotton *yukata* (bath-robe) and from
the glistening black hair, both contrasting
with the girl's white skin and her almost
impassive expression.

36

35 Shinsui Itō

The scent of water
From the first series 'A Collection of
Today's Beauties'
1930. From a limited edition of 250
Woodblock, 427 × 276mm
Published by Shōsaburō Watanabe, Tokyo
1946.2.9.084. Bequeathed by Arthur
Morrison. Illustrated page 59

Like the 'Twelve Forms', this series came out
over several years. If at first glance the image
seems close to Renoir, a closer scrutiny
reveals modelling of rocks in an entirely Far
Eastern tradition, while the patterning of
maple leaves falling on the water is an old
theme of Japanese art. The lady is in fact
washing at a hot spring, and this print is
similar in mood to the artist's painting *Pure
Morning* done in the same year, which shows
four girls bathing at Shiohara.

36 Shinsui Itō

Gifu Lantern
From the first series
'A Collection of Today's Beauties'
1930. From a limited edition of 250
Woodblock, 425 × 280mm
Published by Shōsaburō Watanabe, Tokyo
1980.12.27.03. Illustrated page 62

A young woman dressed in a summer
kimono is hanging up a folding paper lantern
of the type which originated in Gifu prefecture.
It is delicately painted with autumn flowers,
and both these and the folds of the lantern,
which are represented by blind-printed
indentations, are printed with a delicacy
which equals any in the past. The printer has
also made a special point of representing
every slat of the *sudare* (bamboo blind) to the
girl's right.

37 Shinsui Itō

Kotatsu
From the second series
'A Collection of Today's Beauties'
1931. From a limited edition of 250
Woodblock, 431 × 282mm
Published by Shōsaburō Watanabe, Tokyo
1980.12.27.09. Illustrated page 63

This print is dated in December, a cold month
in Japan, and it shows a young woman
keeping warm by the device called a *kotatsu*.
This is a charcoal brazier enclosed in a
wooden frame. Over it one draws a quilt
which also covers the lower part of the body.
In this way it is possible to stay warm in the
drafty traditional Japanese house. The
sumptuousness of this image is enhanced by
the powdered mica background.

37

44

40

38 Shinsui Itō

Driving Snow
From the second series
'A Collection of Today's Beauties'
1932. From a limited edition of 250
Woodblock, 434 × 279mm
Published by Shōsaburō Watanabe, Tokyo
1981.8.1.02. Illustrated page 44

A *geisha* on her way to or from an
engagement is caught in a snow flurry, and
provides the subject for one of Shinsui's most
ravishing designs; its sense of movement and
the harmony of its unusually wide range of
colours compensates for that over-sweetness
into which he was apt to fall as he grew
older. This became one of his favourite
subjects for paintings, and his hanging scroll
of *c*.1947 of the same name seems to be
based on this print.

39 Shinsui Itō

Washing the Hair
1953. 59th of a limited edition
Woodblock, 522 × 377mm
Published by the Commission for the
Protection of Cultural Properties, Tokyo;
cut and printed by the Japanese Association
for Publishing Woodblock Prints
1982.11.8.01. Illustrated page 67

This large print was published to mark the
artist's elevation in 1952 to the status of an
'Intangible Cultural Property', and it was
given a mica background, the usual symbol
of a special portrait in the *Ukiyoe* style.
Shinsui supervised the printing himself, the
design being closely modelled on the right-
hand figure in his painted two-fold screen
Tresses (1949). The Japanese title of the print
is also 'Tresses'. The print has a monumental
simplicity which harks back to his earliest
work.

40 Shinsui Itō

Kagamijishi
1950. From a limited edition
Woodblock, 330 × 417mm (image)
Published by Shōsaburō Watanabe, Tokyo
1982.11.11.017. Illustrated page 65

Like most of the artist's late prints, this is
based closely on a painting of the same
name. The original was painted in 1946.
Late in his life Shinsui often reverted to a
simpler, more innocent style which is quite
close to the manner of his first master
Kiyokata and which seems even more
simplified in the woodblock version, although
the use of powdered mica and of blind-
printing is in fact very sophisticated. The
subject is a variation of the lion-dance which
became very popular in the Kabuki theatre in
the late nineteenth century.

30

39

42

41a Shinsui Itō

Yabase
From the series 'Eight Views of Lake Omi'
1917
Woodblock, 217 × 314mm
Published by Shōsaburō Watanabe, Tokyo
1946.2.9.096. Bequeathed by
Arthur Morrison. Illustrated page 56

The 'Eight Views of Lake Omi' were a
traditional set in Japanese art. They combined
famous scenic spots round Lake Biwa (Omi)
near Kyoto with eight artistic themes much
used in earlier Chinese painting – 'Autumn
Moon', 'Lingering Snow', 'Evening Glow',
'Evening Bell', 'Returning Sails', 'Brilliant
Sunset', 'Night Rain' and 'Geese Landing'.
Hiroshige (1797–1858) designed a very
celebrated set on this theme, and the young
Shinsui tried with some success to emulate
his achievement. Here the 'returning sails' at
Yabase are seen through pine trees and a
stone lantern, and the whole scene is
imaginatively touched with sunset orange.

41b Shinsui Itō

Hira
From the series 'Eight Views of Lake Omi'
1917
Woodblock, 227 × 323mm
Published by Shōsaburō Watanabe, Tokyo
1946.2.9.078. Bequeathed by
Arthur Morrison. Illustrated page 57

Mount Hira is usually shown with 'Lingering
Snow', though if there is any snow in this
scene it is concealed with great subtlety. Here
and in some of the other 'Eight Views' the
young Shinsui successfully revived the
mid-nineteenth-century landscape tradition
by grafting on to it some of the techniques
of more recent French art. The austere
simplicities of this windswept view of lake
and mountain still impress with their
freshness and keenly felt atmosphere.

42 Hasui Kawase 1883–1957

Snow at Shirahige
From the series 'Twelve Scenes in Tokyo'
1920. From a limited edition of 200
Woodblock, 268 × 386mm
Published by Shōsaburō Watanabe, Tokyo
1946.2.9.069. Bequeathed by
Arthur Morrison. Illustrated page 68

Hasui, like Shinsui, was a pupil of Kiyokata,
but previous to that he had studied Western-
style painting. Again, like Shinsui, he was
encouraged into designing for the woodblock
print by Watanabe. His unerring eye for the
picturesque in landscape was compensated in
his early years by restraint and can be seen
in this charming riverside view, but it deserted
him as he became more and more celebrated
outside Japan and sought to equal the success
of Hiroshi Yoshida. Here, however, he shows
himself a true successor of the great
landscapist Hiroshige (1797–1858).

43 Hasui Kawase

Rain at Uchisange, Okayama
From the series 'Selected Landscapes'
1923. From a limited edition of 300
Woodblock, 300 × 225 mm
Published by Shōsaburō Watanabe, Tokyo
1946.2.9.071. Bequeathed by
Arthur Morrison. Illustrated page 19

Hasui was a determined traveller, like many
of his countrymen. In this series he records
sights in widely separated parts of Japan in a
small format which keeps his exuberance
within bounds, and it may be considered one
of his most successful. This sombre print of
the castle district of Okayama in western
Honshū sees him at his atmospheric best.

44 Shūhō Yamakawa 1898–1944

Red Collar
1928
Woodblock, 383 × 264 mm
1981.10.21.02. Illustrated page 64

Shūhō was yet another of the pupils of
Kiyokata (Shinsui, Hasui, Kotondo and Shirō
were others) who headed the *Ukiyoe* revival.
He published many of his prints himself. A
rather unobtrusive artist, he has concentrated
on that old Japanese erotic standby, the back
of the neck, with a few tantalisingly loose
hairs straying down, and only a partial view
of the woman's face. In the true tradition of
Ukiyoe, too, Shūhō concentrates most of the
emotional impact into the careful and fine
depiction of the fabrics, the hair comb and
the coiffure, enhanced by a sprinkled mica
background.

45 Kotondo Torii 1900–1977

Rain
1929. From a limited edition of 300
Woodblock, 383 × 264 mm
Published by Sakai and Kawaguchi, Tokyo;
printed by Komatsu; blocks cut by Itō
1981.10.21.02. Illustrated page 69

Kotondo belonged to the Torii family which
since the late seventeeth century had
specialised in prints of the Kabuki theatre.
In the late 1920s, however, he designed
prints of beautiful women which are rated
second only to Shinsui's in that generation.
His style, notwithstanding his reputation,
tends to lack bite, and only a few of his prints
carry much force. This is perhaps the best
known. It shows an elegant woman sheltering
from the rain under a waxed paper umbrella.
The rain is represented, as in the old *Ukiyoe*
convention, by straight white lines.

45

47

63a

竹久夢二木版画集

63b

46 Hiroaki Takahashi 1871–1945

Awabi fisher
*c.*1936
Woodblock, 530 × 365 mm
Published by the Fusui Gabō, Tokyo
1982.1.25.01. Illustrated page 49

The women who dived for Awabi shells were
much appreciated in pre-modern Japan
because of their reputation for passion. The
great *Ukiyoe* artist Utamaro (1753–1806)
designed some memorable prints of them.
Takahashi has revived this tradition in a
large, mica-ground print which owes part of
its inspiration to the work of Goyō. The
publisher Fusui Shobō specialised in prints
which recreated the paintings of the great
Ukiyoe artists of the past. This design shows
the traditional wet hair, while to avoid the
censor's disapproval instead of the seaweed
used by earlier artists Takahashi has cleverly
suggested it in the ragged tassels of the girl's
towel. (For Takahashi, see also no. 68.)

47 Inshō Dōmoto 1891–1975

New Year Toilette
1935. 7th of a limited edition
Woodblock, 507 × 375 mm
Published by Baba Nobuhiko, Kyoto.
Printed by Satō, blocks cut by Katsumura
1981.4.10.05. Illustrated page 69

In this very luxurious print a young woman
is seen putting a pin into her New Year
coiffure. Her kimono is decorated with plum
blossoms and pine fronds, both symbols of
the New Year. Inshō was a varied and
eccentric artist who worked mainly on
paintings for Buddhist temples, and most of
his extant prints are also of Buddhist subjects;
but here he designed a work in the detailed
and opulent *Ukiyoe* style of the eighteenth
and nineteenth centuries.

49

53

54

49 Shunsen Natori 1886–1960

Portrait of the actor Ennosuke Ichikawa in the part of Kakudayū
1927. From a limited edition of 150
Woodblock, 390 × 272mm
Published by Shōsaburō Watanabe, Tokyo
1966.6.13.04. Illustrated page 73

Shunsen, together with Kampō, was the best of the artists who headed the third thrust of the *Ukiyoe* revival of the period from 1915 onwards, that of portraits of the still very popular Kabuki actors. Of these Ennosuke of the old Ichikawa family was one of the most eminent. He is seen here as the robber Kakudayū, his head sinisterly shaved, his face contorted in one of the set expressions which are one of the Kabuki actor's skills.

50 Shunsen Natori

Portrait of the actor Kōshirō Matsumoto in the part of Ikyū
1929. From a limited edition of 100
Woodblock, 404 × 270mm
Published by Shōsaburō Watanabe, Tokyo
1981.10.21.04. Illustrated page 18

This elaborate portrait is from the very popular play, *Sukeroku*, written in 1713. It is a story of villainy overcome by an *otokodate*, a hero from the lower levels of society. The villain, Ikyū, is a tyrannical old samurai celebrated for his long white beard (an unusual feature when the play was written), and the printer has used blind-printing to represent it. He is seen drawing his sword which features dramatically at the end of the play.

51 Shunsen Natori

Portrait of the actor Enjaku Jitsukawa in the part of Danshichi
1926. 114th from a limited edition of 150
Woodblock, 401 × 275mm
Published by Shōsaburō Watanabe, Tokyo
1982.11.11.014. Illustrated page 52

The original wrapper states that the blocks were destroyed at the end of the edition. This magnificent design in blue and red, using both the actor's costume and a patterned curtain behind him, is one of the artist's masterpieces in actor portraits. Danshichi Kurobei is the hero of *Natsu Matsuri* ('The Summer Festival'), a popular *sewamono*, or 'common people's play', of a violent nature. He represents the noble aspirations of the ordinary townsfolk during the repressive Edo period.

48 Kiyosada Torii 1844–1901 and Kiyotada Torii 1875–1941

The actor Danjūrō Ichikawa IX (1842–1903) in the role of Narukami with a female impersonator as Taemahime
From a portfolio of the 'Eighteen Plays'
1926–7
Woodblock, 348 × 273mm
Published by Shūjirō Oana at Shūbisha, Tokyo; printed by Kin'ei Itō
1981.7.30.01 (13). Illustrated page 72

The 'Eighteen Plays' were a collection selected by Danjūrō VII in 1840 of the best *aragoto* ('rough stuff') plays in the repertory of the Ichikawa family. Danjūrō IX, much the most famous actor of his age, was still remembered with awe a generation later, as this very traditional-style *Ukiyoe* print shows. The portfolio seems to have been designed by Kiyotada using original sketches by his father Kiyosada, who was a contemporary of Danjūrō IX.

The play *Narukami* is about a man who kidnapped the rain-god and was outwitted by the seductive Taemahime. The portfolio came out in nine monthly parts of two prints each in a folder. This example is from Part 7.

52 Shunsen Natori

*The actor Sōjurō Sawamura
in the part of Reizō Narihira*
1927. From a limited edition of 150
Woodblock, 405 × 275mm
Published by Shōsaburō Watanabe, Tokyo
1973.7.23.02. Given by R.E. Lewis.
Illustrated page 53

The stage properties in the Kabuki theatre
have always been used to great effect. Shunsen
has seized on the splendid umbrella carried
by Narihira to protect him from the snow
and used it to concentrate attention on the
actor's compelling face and to form a contrast
between its yellow and brown bands and the
rich blue of the actor's outer coat. Shunsen,
like all the great Kabuki portraitists, had the
ability to convey the actor's own personality
through the make-up and the set expressions.

53 Shunsen Natori

*Portrait of the actor
Kichiemon Nakamura in the part of
Mitsuhide*
1925. From a limited edition of 150
Woodblock, 403 × 280mm
Published by Shōsaburō Watanabe, Tokyo
1981.10.21.05. Illustrated page 73

The whorling marks of the *baren* (printer's
pad) fill the background of this portrait with
turbulence, as befits the troubled mood of the
treacherous Akechi Mitsuhide who plotted to
murder the sixteenth-century statesman and
soldier Nobunaga. The play in which this
part occurs in *Ehon Taikōki* ('The Picture-
Book of the Taikō'), written in 1799. The
Taikō is the title of Hideyoshi, Nobunaga's
lieutenant who hastened to attack Mitsuhide.

54 Kampō Yoshikawa 1894–

*The actor Gadō Kataoka in the part of
Miyuki*
1924. From a limited edition of 200
Woodblock, 416 × 275mm
Published by Shōtarō Satō, Kyoto; printed by
Oiwa; blocks cut by Maeda
1981.10.21.06. Illustrated page 76

Kampō was a man of the Kabuki theatre in
three ways – as adviser to the prominent
Shōchiku Company, as designer of actors'
portraits, and as writer. Like many of his
great predecessors he excelled in the
ambiguities of the *onnagata*, the men who
had played female roles in Kabuki since the
mid-seventeenth century. Miyuki in the play
Shōutsushi Asagao Nikki ('The Diary of
Morning Glory') is the daughter of a wealthy
samurai whose head-cover blows off at a
boating party and leads to her meeting and
falling in love with the hero. She is seen here
wearing plectra on her fingers for playing the
koto.

55

55 Kampō Yoshikawa

*The actor Ganjirō Nakamura in the
part of Jihei Kamiya*
1922. From a limited edition of 200
Woodblock, 410 × 272mm
Published by Shōtarō Satō, Kyoto;
printed by Oiwa; blocks cut by Maeda
1973.7.23.07. Illustrated page 77

The drama in which this part is played is
Kamiji, also known as *Shinjū Tennō Amijima*
('The Love Suicide At Amijimá'). It is the
most famous of the works of Chikamatsu,
Japan's greatest playwright, and was written
c.1715. Its popularity was due to its stark
conflict of passion and duty, a situation
which went straight to the hearts of the
Japanese. Jihei, a respectably married paper-
merchant, was led to a double suicide with
the courtesan Koharu by such a conflict.

56

56 Toyonari Yamamura

1886–1942

Portrait of the actor Sonosuke in the part of Umegawa

1922. From a limited edition of 150
Woodblock, 425 × 285 mm
1973.7.23.010. Illustrated page 80

Toyonari (who used the art-name Kōka in his paintings) was taught by Gekkō Ogata, and thus was in a direct line from the traditional artists of the past. He produced only a few actor portraits, many of them published by himself, but they all have a lurid sense of drama which makes them easily recognisable. This example with its mica background and simple power is a worthy successor to the great actor portraits of Sharaku (fl. 1794–5), who too excelled in studies of female impersonators. The character here is the courtesan Umegawa in the popular tragic play *Umegawa-Chūbei* written by Chikamatsu *c*.1706.

Between two worlds

57 Bakusen Tsuchida 1887–1936

'A young *maiko*'

From the book *Bakusen Gashū*
('Bakusen's Picture Collection')
1921. This copy signed by the artist,
20 August 1921
Woodblock, 433 × 331 mm
Published by the artist at Benridō, Kyoto;
printed by Jizaemon Nakamura
1982.7.29.01. Illustrated page 80

In spite of being dedicated to the memory of Seihō's parents, this *de-luxe* book, printed on hand-made paper incorporating watermarks of the artist's name, was an ambitious act of self-advertisement by Bakusen. It includes collotypes of some of his best-known paintings in the *Nihonga* ('Japanese Painting') style, some decorative woodblocks in the text, and three large woodblocks reproducing his colour sketches of Kyoto *maiko* in a much more Westernised style. These sketches were for a screen he painted in 1919. The paper cover of the book is also adorned with a very attractive woodblock after a study of poppies.

58 Gesson Okamoto 1876–1931

'Deck listening'

From Volume 2 of the book *Gesson Gashū*
(Gesson's Picture Collection)
1934. 21st of a limited edition
Line block, 133 × 152 mm (image)
Published by the 'Society to Publish the

57

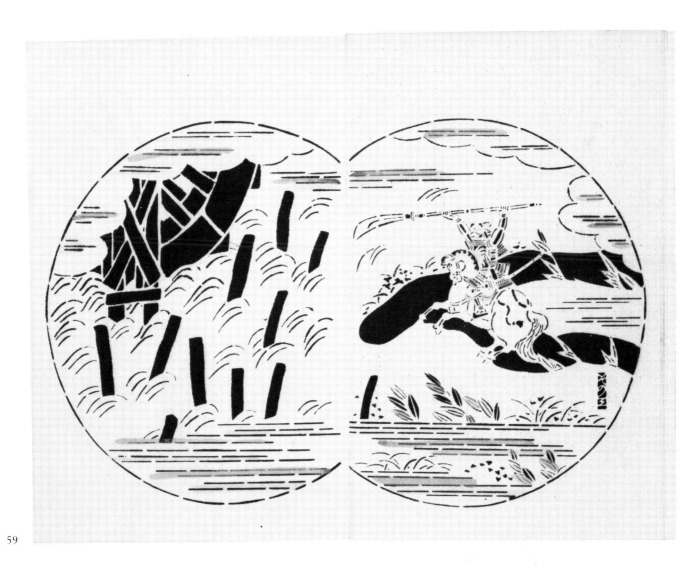

59

Book' under the supervision of Karube Yasuo at Daruma Bookshop, Okayama; blocks engraved by Ise, Igarashi, Nakanishi and Kawanaka; printed by Tōhachi Yotsuya 1980.12.27.020/1. Illustrated page 20

This memorial book to the semi-Westernised illustrator and artist Gesson is unusual in being in line block, mostly in black and white, but with a few colour plates tipped in, and also in being in two contrasting volumes of the same size, the first upright in format and the second horizontal.

59 Keisuke Serizawa 1895–

'Don Quixote tilts at a watermill'
From the book *Ehon Don Kihōte*
1936. 17th of a limited edition of 100
Stencil, 285 × 370mm (double page)
Published by the Sunward Press, Kyoto
1973.7.23.0151. Illustrated page 81

Serizawa, one of the giants of the Folk Art movement, revived the art of stencil-printing illustrated books which had flourished in the seventeenth and early eighteenth centuries in

the Osaka and Kyoto areas. He produced many books in his productive life. This charming volume tells the story of Don Quixote in the shape of a medieval Japanese warrior. The style is also of the Japanese Middle Ages as continued in the popular books of the seventeenth century, as is the simple colouring in black, green, yellow and orange.

60 Tsuguji Fujita (Leonard Foujita) 1886–1968

Self-portrait
*c.*1922. Artist's proof
Etching, 395 × 260mm (image)
1949.4.11.2453. Bequeathed by
Campbell Dodgson. Illustrated page 84

Fujita is the only Japanese artist to have worked outside Japan for a long period and to have achieved there a high reputation. He worked in France from 1913 to 1929 and frequently visited that country thereafter, finally becoming a French citizen in 1955. He was also a Roman Catholic convert, as the crucifix in this etching emphasises. Western though the technique and style are, there is a simple intensity about the artist's self-contemplation which comes from his Japanese personality.

昭和二八年作

姫路城

霞む夕べ
——不忍池畔——

昭和七年春、笠松紫浪

77

60

62

61 Tsuguji Fujita (Leonard Foujita)

Portrait of a European woman
c.1935
Woodblock, 427 × 295mm
Published by the Katō Hanga Kenkyūjo,
Tokyo
1980.12.27.013(A). Illustrated page 79

The publisher Katō specialised in prints after
the more Westernised artists but he did them
in a strictly traditional woodblock technique.
Nevertheless, he succeeded remarkably well
in reproducing the thin, elegant line and
clear, pale colours of Fujita's painting in the
French style. This line, itself originally a
Japanese feature, was much admired in
France and can be particularly appreciated in
this lady's sinuous fingers. There is also an
oblique, mysterious quality in this portrait
which is more Japanese than French and
which the disarming simplicity of the
woodblock medium only emphasises.

62 Tsuguji Fujita (Leonard Foujita)

Akita girl
1937
Woodblock, 370 × 262mm
Published by the Katō Hanga Kenkyūjo,
Tokyo
1980.12.27.013(B). Illustrated page 84

This apparently 'primitive' print is signed in
Japanese 'At Akita, Tsuguji' and in English
'Foujita 1937'. It is typical of the stolid
nationalism to which even a refined artist
such as Fujita could fall prey as Japan slid
towards war, and stands in surprising contrast
to nos 60 and 61. The girl is a representative
of the solid and unimaginative virtues of the
peasants of the north of Honshū with its
long, snowbound winters, and the heavy
folky colours, so different from the artist's
normal palette, emphasise a startling change
of sentiment.

66

春の夜―銀座

昭和九年四月

69

63a Yumeji Takehisa 1884–1934

Tatsutahime
From 'A collection of Takehisa Yumeji's
pictures in woodblock prints'
*c.*1935
Woodblock, 512 × 390mm
Published by the Kyōto Hanga-in
(Dai Edo Han); printed by Itakura; blocks cut
by Endō. This print is based on a painted
two-fold screen done in 1931
1982.10.7.010. Illustrated page 70

Tatsutahime is a Shintō goddess of the
harvest, and Yumeji, at a time of deep
economic depression, playfully dedicated this
picture to her depicted against a barren view
of Mount Fuji in the hope of better times.
He is recorded as saying that the lady was
'Miss Nippon', and certainly she has more
than her share of that *Japonisme* which late
nineteenth-century Europeans invented.

The inscription, adapted from a verse of
the Tang poet Du Fu, translates 'Last year
the rice was dear and there was more for
eating; this year it is cheap and the farmers
are in trouble; dedicated to Tatsutahime, a
poem by Du (Fu)'.

63b Yumeji Takehisa

Frog
From the same series as no. 63
1982.10.7.011. Illustrated page 71

This bewilderingly titled print is based on a
hanging painting done in 1930 of which the
top section showing an overhanging bough
of a tree has been left out. The outdoor
atmosphere is therefore missing.

64 Yumeji Takehisa

Woman's hood
1938. 46th of a limited portfolio of 150
Woodblock, 440 × 310mm
Published by Junji Katō, Tokyo
1981.7.30.07. Illustrated page 78

Katō (who also published Fujita's works)
produced woodblock prints of a number of
Yumeji's paintings and sketches after his
death. Particularly good are the prints after
the pastels which the artist did in the early
1920s when he was still light-hearted and
entranced with the exotic Western fashions
and styles of the years after the First World
War. This lady seems particularly Westernised,
especially in her make-up and head-on stare,
but there is no reason to doubt that she was
in fact Japanese.

65 Yumeji Takehisa

The Tanabata Festival
A design for the dinner menu of the
M.S. *Asama Maru*
1929
Woodblock, 370 × 240mm
1981.10.23.01. Illustrated page 21

This delightful trifle is comparatively unusual
in Yumeji's work, for it was designed specially
for the woodblock medium. After the prints
he designed and supervised himself in the
years 1914–16, which are extremely rare, he
did little graphic work, and most prints are in
fact after his paintings. The simplicity of this
study of a woman hanging a lantern at the
July Tanabata Festival is closer to his early
print style and his hot palette, though the
composition is related to his painted screen
on the same subject done in 1923. The
colours include powdered gold, and the menu
itself is decorated with pine needles printed in
green and brown.

66 Toraji Ishikawa 1875–1964

After the bath
1934
Woodblock, 480 × 372 mm
Blocks cut by Kazue Yamagishi
1981.7.30.02. Illustrated page 85

Ishikawa was best known as a painter in a mixed Japanese and European style, following a period of study in France early in the century. Some of his prints were made after his paintings, but his series of nude women produced in 1934 was specially designed for the woodcut medium. The blocks were cut by another minor print artist, Yamagishi. In this group the artist shows the very strong influence of contemporary French art, particularly in the dumpy, unidealised bodies, and this impression is increased by the short hairstyles then favoured by fashionable Japanese women. The scene, however, is entirely traditional – a woman drying herself by the side of the bath, probably in an *onsen* (hot spring resort).

67 Toraji Ishikawa

Leisure hours
1934
Woodblock, 372 × 468 mm
Blocks cut by Kazue Yamagishi
1981.5.25.01. Illustrated page 75

In a rather more modern vein than no. 66 Ishikawa depicts a nude woman looking at a woodblock book of fashionably dressed and coiffured women. Thus the artist links himself with the *Ukiyoe* school of printmakers. However, there is also a touch of satire in the contrast, and in the implied comparison with the very soundly sleeping cat.

68 Hiroaki Takahashi 1871–1944

Belled cat
c.1935
Woodblock, 273 × 392 mm
Published by the Fusui Gabō, Tokyo
1983.3.12.05. Illustrated page 22

This extraordinary print gives a strongly 'Western' impression, but it is not in fact close to any Western model, and the techniques used are almost aggressively traditional. The black of the cat is 'lacquered' by adding a glue to the ink, a throw-back to a method of the early eighteenth century for luxury prints. The cat's shadow, the only really foreign pictorial element, is nevertheless expressed with a grey block showing the exaggerated mark of the printer's *baren* (rubbing pad), and the yellow background shows these whorling marks even more clearly (see also no. 46).

71

72

昭和十三年　夜の東京　屋台店

夜の水都 両國橋より 昭和十四年 田舎

From the Ryogoku Bridge — Yoshida

73

69 Kampō Yoshikawa 1894–

Early Morning Mist at Sanjō Ōhashi
1924. From of a limited edition of 200
Woodblock, 277 × 405mm
Published by Shōtarō Satō, Kyoto; printed by
Ōiwa; blocks cut by Maeda
1981.3.30.01. Illustrated page 88

A very atmospheric view in the centre of
Kyoto, this print nevertheless shows the
marked influence of recent French graphics
in its diagonal construction and in its quiet
colours. Only grey, black and blue are used.
It is a surprising work from an artist who
specialised in Kabuki portraits (see nos 54–5).
This example is personally signed by Kampō
in the margin and dedicated to 'Mr Henry H.
Hart', a collector of *Ukiyoe* prints.

70 Kazuma Oda 1882–1956

The Great Bridge at Matsue
1924
Woodblock, 235 × 460mm (image)
Published by Shōsaburō Watanabe, Tokyo
1982.11.11.015. Illustrated page 74

Oda was one of the founders of the *Sōsaku
Hanga* movement and was thought of as very
Westernised. This is probably because he did
so much lithography, for which he is best
known, but the style is in fact a mixture not
very far removed from other *Shin Hanga*
landscapists such as Hasui, Shirō and Kōitsu,
and this is all the clearer in the woodblocks
of his work published by Watanabe. In this
very effective work he contrasts a shifting,
distorted background with a very traditional
group of women in the foreground. Matsue is
on the cold, unwelcoming north-west coast
of Honshū.

71 Kazuma Oda

Mihonoseki in Izumo
1925. From a limited edition of 100
Woodblock, 365 × 243mm (image)
Published by Shōsaburō Watanabe, Tokyo
1983.3.12.04. Illustrated page 89

Another print of the bleak north-west coast,
this too combines a very Japanese
atmosphere and technique with elements of
Western structure. The most noticeable of
them is the view straight down on the boats
moored in the immediate foreground, a
feature found in several *Sōsaku Hanga*
compositions such as Hakutei's *Log Rafts*. The
rather languid placing of the figure in the
building to the left also savours of
contemporary French composition and of the
curious mixture of relaxation and tension in
Japan in the 1920s.

74

72 Konen Uehara 1878–1940

Dōtonbori
1928
Woodblock, 362 × 240mm
Published by Shōsaburō Watanabe, Tokyo
1983.3.12.06. Illustrated page 89

This delightful view in the pleasure quarter of Osaka is one of the few known prints by Konen, a pupil of Kajita (see no. 1). It shows a great house of entertainment across the canal, seen in heavy rain and through a network of willow trees which overhang the water. Most of the print is done in black and grey, with slight tones of pink and yellow. It is these points of light in the darkness more than the composition itself which give a Westernised impression.

73 Hasui Kawase 1883–1957

Banyu River
1931. From a limited edition of 200
Woodblock, 240 × 360mm (image)
Published by Shōsaburō Watanabe, Tokyo
1946.2.9.072. Bequeathed by Arthur Morrison. Illustrated page 92

In prints such as these Hasui showed his stronger and stronger leanings towards the sort of picturesqueness with which Hiroshi Yoshida had had such success, and at which he was to prove equally adept (no. 81). The distant view of Mount Fuji, shrouded in elaborate effects of mist and cloud, is scenic in a very Western way, and contrasts sharply with his earlier works (nos 42–3) which were more in the vein of Shinsui. Hasui's new-found skill – skyscape – was to prove a key to his commercial success.

74 Hasui Kawase

Temple gateway in spring
1940
Woodblock, 267 × 395mm
1980.12.27.011. Illustrated page 93

The publisher is probably Watanabe of Tokyo, who did almost all Hasui's prints. Increasingly prolific through the 1930s, the artist found a ready market for his Japanese views in a country which was passing through a period of extreme nationalism. Not a sign of the modern world of industry and war, in which Japan was in 1940 so wholeheartedly participating, can be detected in this scene of a Kyoto temple, yet there is a sobriety lurking in the subdued tones.

Sinjuku

Toshi Yoshida

83

94

Shrine of the Paper-Makers, Fukui

Toshi Yoshida

一九五一年作

岡太神社

76

75 Kōitsu Ishiwata 1897–

At Katsushika Sankaku

1931
Woodblock, 390 × 260 mm
Published by Shōsaburō Watanabe, Tokyo
1981.10.21.01. Illustrated page 97

Kōitsu is one of the most attractive of the minor landscape artists who flourished in the 1930s. A pupil of Hasui, he avoided the master's over-prettiness and sometimes grandiose scenery, and instead produced small-scale views of towns and villages with all their clutter and with a very strong affection for the minutiae of traditional life. This view of a country food-shop and noodle restaurant is far from idealised, and it clearly omits no detail from the sketches made by the sharp-eyed artist.

76 Kōitsu Ishiwata

View at Koyasuhama, Kanagawa

1931
Woodblock, 386 × 266 mm
Published by Shōsaburō Watanabe, Tokyo
1981.10.21.03. Illustrated page 96

Kōitsu's fondness for ordinary life is very evident in this study of a barber's shop at a small town in Kanagawa prefecture (just to the south-west of Tokyo). He has picked a scene which is not only in the night but also in the rain, and he has restricted his colours virtually to black and yellow alone to suggest the little pool of human comfort in the darkness. In spite of its nationalism, this print shows how utterly assimilated the Western techniques of light and shade had become.

77 Shirō Kasamatsu 1898–

Misty evening at Shinobazu pond

1932
Woodblock, 385 × 362 mm
Published by Shōsaburō Watanabe, Tokyo
1946.2.9.06. Bequeathed by Arthur Morrison. Illustrated page 83

Shirō studied under Kaburagi Kiyokata, who also inspired Shinsui and Hasui. All three became excellent landscapists, in spite of their master's preference for female subjects. During the 1930s Shirō became one of the minor landscape masters encouraged, published and sold by Watanabe. It would be more accurate to describe him as a townscapist, for it is street and indoor scenes at which he excelled. This view of a favourite resort of Tokyoites is very romanticised; it reflects partly the Western view of picturesque Japan.

Holding on to the past

78 Shirō Kasamatsu

*Morning at the Spa: Nozawa
in Shinano*
1933
Woodblock, 387 × 262mm
Published by Shōsaburō Watanabe, Tokyo
1946.2.9.085. Bequeathed by Arthur
Morrison. Illustrated page 98

One of the favourite Japanese leisure activities
has for long been to visit the hot-spring
resorts. Nozawa, in the mountains in modern
Nagano prefecture (formerly called Shinano),
is one of the most famous, and has many
public baths of the sort shown in this print,
its roof partly open to the sky in summer
because of the high temperature of the
natural water. Like Shinsui in no. 32, Shirō
has used the marks of the printer's pad
(*baren*) to produce the effect of steam.

79 Shirō Kasamatsu

*Spring Snow – the Shimakoshi Shrine
at Asakusa*
1934
Woodblock, 394 × 263mm
Published by Shōsaburō Watanabe, Tokyo
1981.10.10.01. Illustrated page 24

On her nocturnal visit to the Shintō shrine
the woman carries a small offering, probably
of rice. She is accompanied by a little girl.
Both are in formal dress for this visit to the
kami, perhaps to ask favours, and both wear
the high clogs (*geta*) which protect them from
the snow. The melancholy and inwardness of
this cold and dark scene are relieved only by
the light of the shrine, a symbol of Japan's
national religion which was to play such a
strong role in the push towards war.

80 Shirō Kasamatsu

*The Great Lantern at the Asakusa
Kannondō*
1934. From a limited edition of 100
Woodblock, 360 × 240mm (image)
1981.2.25.04(A). Illustrated page 86

The 'Kannon Hall' is part of the Sensōji
Temple in Asakusa, a fairly Bohemian district
of Tokyo before the Second World War. It is
famous for its huge paper lantern, of which
Hiroshige had done a celebrated print in his
One Hundred Views of Edo in the late 1850s.
Shirō's view is similarly constructed to
Hiroshige's, but its rather pessimistic, dark
atmosphere is noticeably different from the
early master's cheerful and light-filled
version. As often in this artist's work, the
figures have their backs to us.

90

88a

96

81 Hiroshi Yoshida 1876–1950

Himeji Castle: Evening
1928
Woodblock, 387 × 263 mm
1946.2.9.073. Bequeathed by Arthur
Morrison. Illustrated page 82

Yoshida was in his day the most successful of
all Japanese artists, especially in the USA
where he was the star of two great *Shin
Hanga* exhibitions in 1930 and 1936 in
Toledo. Originally a landscape painter in the
Western style, he was persuaded by
Watanabe to design for prints about 1920
but soon became so celebrated that he began
to publish his own prints. The Yoshida family
have done this ever since. This romantic
view of Japan's most portrayed castle is
characteristic of the work which earned him
international acceptance.

82 Shirō Kasamatsu

Spring Night – Ginza
1934
Woodblock, 393 × 263 mm
Published by Shōsaburō Watanabe, Tokyo
1981.2.25.03(B). Illustrated page 87

In the foreground is a stall selling *sushi* (a
dish of cold rice, fish or vegetables and
seaweed), and in the middle ground a lantern
advertising the spring theatre performances.
The background is filled by the very typical
between-the-Wars buildings of the Tokyo
entertainment area. Among these inanimate
features the people, in a mixture of Western
and Japanese dress, seem shadowy and
uncertain. Shirō was in the 1930s very
sensitive to this introverted atmosphere and
has recorded it with a poetic skill which he
never regained after the catastrophe of the
War.

83 Tōshi Yoshida 1911–

Shinjuku
1938. From the series 'Tokyo at Night'
Woodblock, 268 × 200 mm
1981.2.25.02(B). Illustrated page 94

The son of Hiroshi Yoshida, Tōshi has since
his father's death carried on the family
reputation for prolific, beautifully produced
woodblocks of the scenery of Japan, and
increasingly of the whole world. He has also
written and lectured extensively on
traditional techniques. Like his father, he
publishes his own works, supervising the
printing and sometimes cutting the blocks.
This series 'Tokyo at Night' (see also nos 84
and 85) is perhaps his masterpiece. It was
done in a small format in the last years
before the War, and has an unpretentious
sense of nostalgia which is most attractive.

97　　　柿の木　　　　　休泉はま　　　　　　　　　　　　　Joichi Hoshi '76

91a

91b

99

84 Tōshi Yoshida

Supper Waggon
1938. From the series 'Tokyo at Night'
Woodblock, 195 × 265 mm
1981.2.25.03(A). Illustrated page 90

This scene is one which even today can be seen in the streets of Tokyo at night. Small booths, covered only by printed cotton curtains, sell bowls of soup or noodles, often at very low prices, to passers-by. Among the foods advertised in this keenly observed print are *sushi, udon* (fat noodles in soup) and meat dishes. A woman carries her child on her back in the traditional manner. It is difficult to reconcile this scene with a nation mobilising for an aggressive war.

85 Tōshi Yoshida

From the Ryōgoku Bridge
1939. From the series 'Tokyo at Night'
Woodblock, 200 × 220 mm
1981.2.25.03(B). Illustrated page 91

This print is the darkest and grimmest of the whole series, and one in which the austere and pessimistic mood of Japan can most clearly be felt. It is astonishing to compare this work with the artist's often garish mountain scenes of more recent years. Ironically, the Ryōgoku Bridge was once the centre of a light-hearted entertainment district and featured in many extrovert prints of the eighteenth and early nineteenth centuries.

86 Tōshi Yoshida

Shrine of the Paper-Makers, Fukui
1951
Woodblock, 407 × 268 mm
1981.2.25.01. Illustrated page 95

The austere, inward-looking atmosphere of the 1930s and 40s continued to be expressed by Japanese artists up to the end of the American occupation. Only after that did a new confidence begin to appear. In this print of 1951 Yoshida conveys through his subdued colours the continued introversion which had its core in the Shintō religion and its shrines. Nevertheless, he was also no doubt moved by visiting the shrine to those craftsmen in paper who were essential to the profession of printmaking.

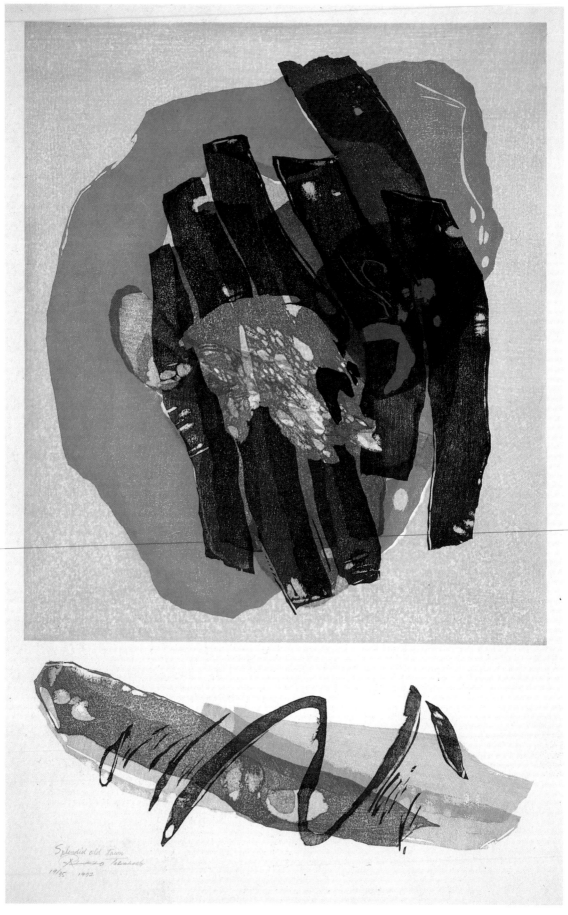

Splendid old Town
Kimazo [signature]
19/25   1992

98

87 Sumio Kawakami 1895–1972

Night of Ginza

From the portfolio 'Scenes of Last Tokyo'
(*Tōkyō Kaigan Zue*)
1946
Woodblock, 183 × 242 mm
Published by Fugaku Honsha, Tokyo; printed
by Takamizawa
1980.12.27.018. Illustrated page 36

This portfolio of fifteen prints expresses an
intense nostalgia for their haunts of pre-war
Tokyo which had just been destroyed; nine
leading *Sōsaku Hanga* artists of the Japanese
Print Association contributed to it.
Kawakami's view of Ginza in the 1920s
is the most memorable and the most lurid.
The other artists were Onchi, Hiratsuka,
Yamaguchi, Maeda, Saitō, Sekino, Azechi
and Maekawa, and most allowed the
bleakness of the present to distort the images
of the past.

88a Kōshirō Onchi 1891–1955

Cherry blossom time (Tokyo)

From the portfolio 'Woman's Customs in
Japan' (*Nihon Jozokusen*)
1946
Woodblock, 242 × 183 mm
Published by Fugaku Honsha, Tokyo; printed
by Takamizawa
1980.12.20.017. Illustrated page 101

A companion set to nos 87 and 89, the
artists of the prints were Onchi, Maekawa,
Kawanishi, Sekino and Saitō, and all were
from the same association. The text, in
English and Japanese, lays great emphasis on
the simple beauty of the Japanese female
dress, and one may speculate on the
direction in which the American occupiers
were being gently led.

88b Kōshirō Onchi

After the bath (Tokyo)

From the same portfolio as 88a
Woodblock, 242 × 183 mm
1980.12.20.017. Illustrated page 40

A geisha is seen emerging from a public bath.
Onchi's native sophistication cannot help
glinting through what is supposed to be a
'pin-up'.

102

89 Jun'ichirō Sekino 1914–

An Oiran's street procession
From the portfolio 'Native Customs in Japan'
(*Nihon Minzoku Zufu*)
1946
Woodblock, 242 × 183 mm
Published by Fugaku Honsha, Tokyo; printed
by Takamizawa
1980.12.27.019. Illustrated page 24

The third portfolio in this series (see nos 87
and 88), its text is the most explicit, claiming
'At this time of change, it may be interesting
to look back (at) the native customs and
festivals as to realise the future image of
Japan'. The artists of the twelve prints are
Maekawa, Mori, Saitō, Sekino, Kawanishi,
Azechi, Kuroki, Maeda, Wakayama and
Yamaguchi. Sekino's sardonic view of a
grand prostitute's procession is borne out by
the publisher's description of it as 'gorgeous
yet puerile manners of the old Japan'.

90 Kōshirō Onchi

'Mount Fuji in Autumn'
From the book *Fresh Praise of Fuji*
1946
Woodblock, 289 × 201 mm (page)
Published by Fugaku Honsha, Tokyo
1979.3.5.390. Illustrated page 100

Like nos 87–9, this book shows a desire to
return to the inner preoccupations of the
Japanese soul. Yuzure Maeda put together
this anthology of his poems in praise of
Japan's peerless mountain in the bitterness of
defeat, and his friend Onchi provided two
haunting woodblocks as illustrations, as well
as a fine design for the paper wrapper.
Although the materials available at that time
were relatively poor, the book was put
together with all the care traditionally
lavished on volumes of poetry. The illustration
shows Fuji under the first snows of autumn.

Dilapidated poetry A 朽ちた詩A   50~1   Hiroyuki Tajima '76

104

5/50   北の海   79.

111

29/50　　　　　　　秋 の 3　　　　　　　—Tokio Miyashita

生死の中の雪ふりしきる

山頭火

扉 IP99　　雪ふりしきる　　秋山巖

92 Kiyoshi Saitō 1907–

Solitude Onrian Kyoto

1955. 86th of an edition of 150
Woodblock, 332 × 478mm
1958.2.8.02. Presented by Sir Stanley Unwin.
Illustrated page 99

Saitō is now one of the 'grand old men' of the
Sōsaku Hanga movement, a position he shares
with Takahashi and Sekino. A single-minded,
rather austere depictor of old Japan's
countryside and buildings, he has since the
mid-1950s achieved great success abroad
among Japanophiles who find his blend of
literalness, abstraction and tasteful simplicity
easy to assimilate. This view of a Kyoto
temple, reduced to strong, simplified blocks, is
an excellent example of his style at its best
before it began to be influenced by his later
fame.

93 Kiyoshi Saitō

Winter in Aizu

c.1965
Woodblock, 290 × 416mm
1980.12.30.02. Illustrated page 25

Saitō, a native of Aizu, has done many scenes
of the hard, snowbound winter of that
mountainous area. Indeed, receding figures
in the snow are his most characteristic
image. Here a peasant is seen wearing the
traditional straw over-cape. Saitō's unusual
technique, born of innocence rather than
originality, of carving multicolour prints from
a single block gives a distinctive sense of
unity to many of his compositions. The
method does encourage sombre colours close
to each other in tone, and in this example
the colours are restricted to black, brown and
grey. It may well be that his many snow
scenes have proved technically easier for the
artist because the white, left in the blank
paper, tends to separate the blocks of colour
which would otherwise run into each other.

94 Gaku Onogi 1924–1976

Landscape (afterimage) C

1968. 9th of an edition of 20
Silk-screen, 300 × 300mm (image)
Illustrated page 26

No photograph even in colour can reproduce
the depth and texture of Onogi's silk-screens
in blue and black, nor their extraordinary
intensity. Most of them, like his oil-paintings,
are called *Landscape*, with or without a more
or less unilluminating subtitle. By contrasting
inks which produced different textures as
well as tones and by the use of heavy
indentation he printed images of luminous
mystery. The refinement of these prints made
very small editions inevitable, and Onogi's
works are already among the rarest of any
recent artist.

Entering the wider world

91a Umetarō Azechi 1902–
'Snowman'

From the book *The Modern Japanese Print*,
1962
1960. 61st of an edition of 510
Woodblock, 418 × 290mm
Published by Tuttle, Tokyo
1981.2.5.01(7). Illustrated page 104

This and 91b are two of the prize-winners
published in Charles Michener's book
(discussed in the Introduction, p. 26). Azechi
was and has remained one of the leading
Sōsaku Hanga artists, inspired always by the
countryside and folk customs of his native
mountains. In this print he neatly reverses
his 'Snowman' into strong colours seen
against a snowy hillside.

91b Sadao Watanabe 1913–

Listening

From the book *The Modern Japanese Print*,
1962
1960. 61st of an edition of 510
Stencil, 478 × 332mm
1981.2.5.01(4). Illustrated page 105

Of all the artists in this book Watanabe (see
no. 106) suffered least from the very large
edition, probably because his technique of
stencil on crumpled paper is less subject to
wear. It is certainly the masterpiece of the
set, and perhaps of the artist.

Old tensions revived

95 Jōichi Hoshi 1913–1979

Treescape E
1975. Artist's proof
Woodblock, 345 × 805 mm
1980.1.28.020. Illustrated page 125

Hoshi was one of the most individual print artists of the post-war period and towards the end of his life concentrated more and more on studies of trees, usually with bare branches. These he did in woodblocks cut by himself which are often masterpieces of the carver's art in themselves. In this exciting example he has used a number of blocks, both blind ones impressed from behind and coloured ones printed from above. The intricate web of branches, done entirely in red, achieves a stately grandeur which is enhanced by the bold point of view cutting off the trunk of the tree. The intense red and the gold-leaf background suggest evening. The composition, horizontally elongated, recalls the shape of a six-fold screen, and could indeed almost be a sketch for a screen in the *Nihonga* (contemporary native Japanese) style.

96 Jōichi Hoshi

Young tree
1975. Artist's proof
Woodblock, 566 × 445 mm
1980.1.28.025. Illustrated page 102 and back cover

Hoshi's late style was capable of extremes of power and delicacy, the latter being evident in this silver birch, which is comparatively rare in his work in being complete with leaves. Although it might be said that the pictorial method is European in origin, the intensity of contemplation of a single tree is a recognisably East Asian tradition.

97 Jōichi Hoshi

Tree at dawn
1976. Artist's proof
Woodblock, 680 × 515 mm
1980.1.28.027. Illustrated page 103

In *Treescape E* (no. 95) Hoshi has cut off the trunk of his tree but has viewed it from high in the air, the favourite point of view of Japanese artists in the traditional schools. Here he looks up at the rootless tree in the manner of Maruyama Ōkyo (1733–95). This great print shows an old, thick-trunked tree, its branches now short and stubby, against a winter dawn. It is perhaps the artist's most intense work, investing the subject with his own feelings as he approached old age. He has enhanced this mood by concentrating attention on the brown and silver mottles of the unusually prominent trunk.

98 Rikio Takahashi 1917–

Splendid Old Town
1972. 19th of an edition of 35
Woodblock, 925 × 608 mm
1981.4.11.08. Illustrated page 108

Takahashi is the most eminent of Onchi's pupils and in one sense the last of the *Sōsaku Hanga* artists descended in an artistic line from Kanae Yamamoto (see Introduction, p. 13. He has explored almost exclusively the abstraction based on natural forms which Onchi was favouring at the end of his life, and also Onchi's favourite technique of imposing blocks partly over each other to produce a wide range of related tones. In spite of the title of this print, its inspiration, as in most of the artist's work, seems to be the traditional Japanese garden, its quiet colours and carefully chosen rocks. In addition, the black ink stroke of the artist and writer's brush is much in evidence.

131

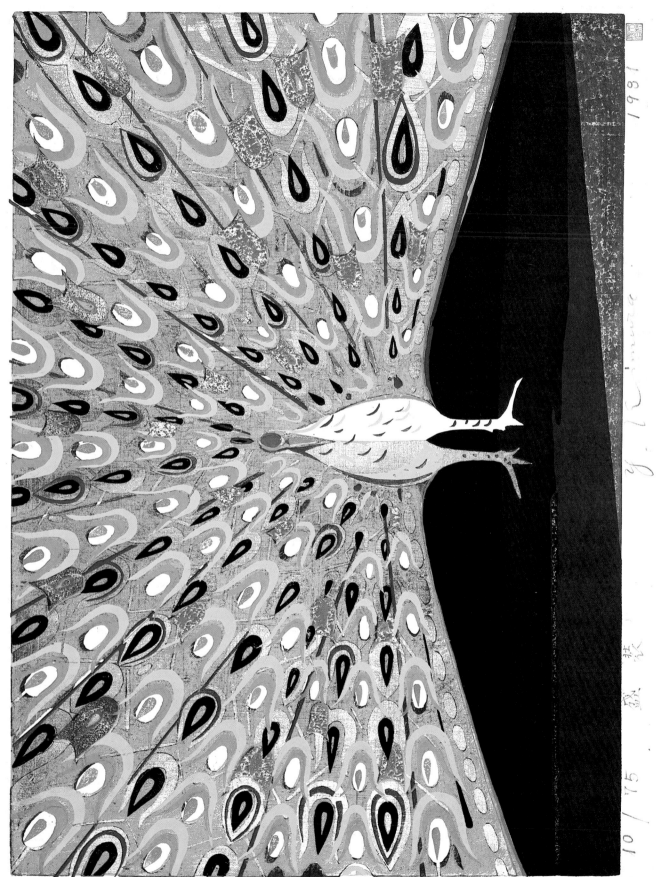

10 / 75 鷲 花 J. K. Chimura 1981

114

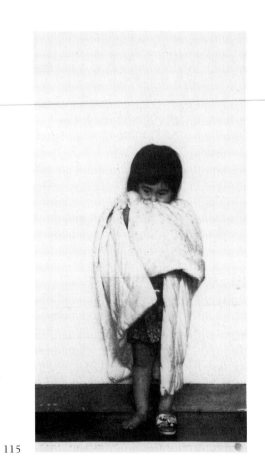

115

116

117

118

119

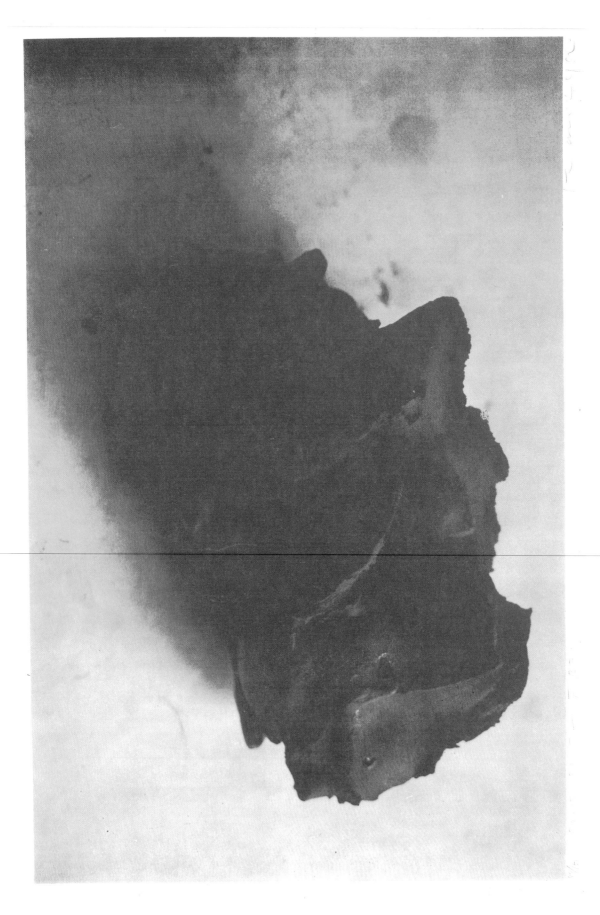

137

120

121

122

123

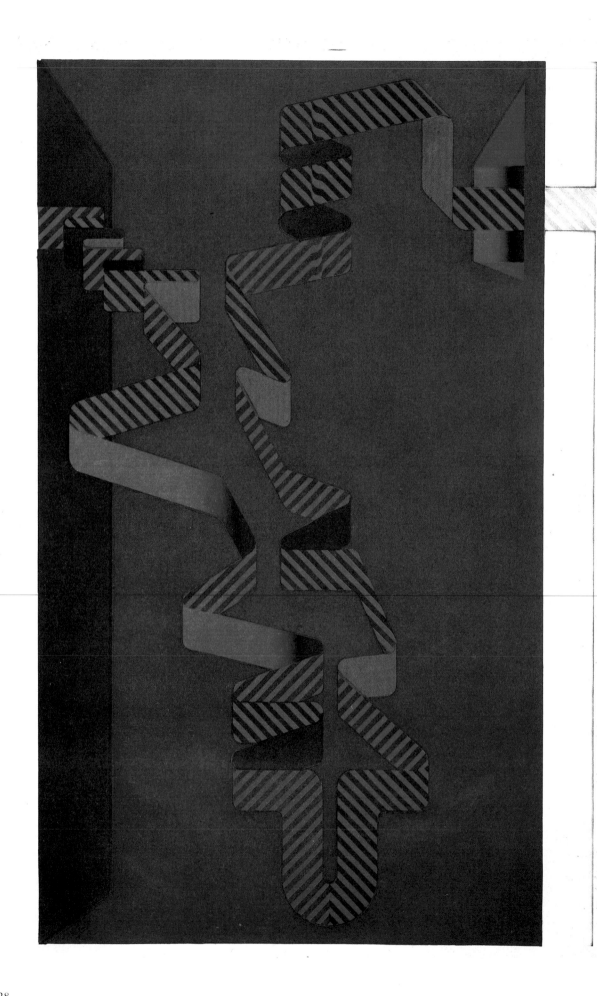

99 Rikio Takahashi 1917–

Nunnery's Garden
No. 49 from the Kyoto series
1975. 21st of an edition of 35
Woodblock, 926 × 607mm
1981.10.13.03. Illustrated page 106

Although a 'conservative' artist, Takahashi was one of the first in the 1960s to expand the format of his prints into some of the biggest done in Japan by the woodblock process. The rather quaint English title refers to the garden of one of Kyoto's many Buddhist *amadera* (convents). It is dominated by warm green and brown tones, but in the detached lower section a carefully selected rock from the garden is printed mainly in its natural grey-black colour.

100 Tōkō Shinoda 1913–

Depth
9th of an edition of 30
Lithograph, with pigments added by hand, 650 × 505mm
1981.10.13.01. Illustrated page 107

Shinoda is one of the most powerful personalities in Japanese art since the Second World War, and in spirit the most masculine. She began as a traditional painter in brush and ink and then turned to lithography (which has been rarely used by Japanese artists) to reproduce graphically the special flavour of her work. In the top central section of this print she has been able through the lithographic plate to represent the 'puddling' of new wet ink on to a still damp area of brushed ink, one of the most refined techniques of the Far Eastern brush. Other ink effects are an edged line (bottom right), 'dry-brush' lines (centre), and thick, matt black (centre). It is significant that Shinoda feels the call of the brush so strongly that she hand-paints additions to her prints.

101 Tōkō Shinoda

Wind from the Sea
13th of an edition of 30
Lithograph, with pigments added by hand, 560 × 730mm
1980.1.28.017. Illustrated page 110

The origins of Shinoda's work in pure Japanese ink painting are abundantly clear in this print. All the energy, force and subtlety of the Japanese brush, used in both calligraphy and painting, can be seen in the sweeping stroke from bottom left to top right. It is remarkable that using the European medium of lithograph and French paper she has succeeded in reproducing the lines of the brush's hairs as they split towards the end of a stroke.

102 Reika Iwami 1927–

February Water
1977. 47th of an edition of 50
Woodblock, 515 × 700mm
1980.1.28.012. Illustrated pages 4–5, 111

Iwami rarely makes a large edition because the pressure required for embossing her prints with 'blind' blocks is so exhausting. This three-dimensional quality is vital to her work, which cannot be properly appreciated through photographs. All her prints incorporate a piece of natural driftwood, symbolising the union of wood with the water which is the usual theme of her work. Like most of her prints, this example is done in shades of black, grey and white, with a little gold leaf representing the moon. The gold is applied in four ways so that the sphere changes its tone when seen from the left or the right. The surging shapes are reminiscent not only of the traditional waves of Japanese art but also of the wave-like forms of rocks as seen in that art.

103 Reika Iwami

Water banquet 79–B
1979. 6th of an edition of 50
Woodblock, 698 × 505mm
1980.1.28.09. Illustrated page 114

Here the driftwood is most effectively used to suggest the surging ocean and to imply a unity between the spheres of the earth, the moon and the sun, the latter represented by gold leaf over an embossed driftwood impression. Like all Iwami's prints, the image is fixed with firm precision, yet also with a delicate refinement which is the artist's most recognisable quality.

104 Hiroyuki Tajima 1911–

Dilapidated Poetry A
1976. 1st of an edition of 50
Woodblock, 633 × 500mm
1980.12.29.08. Illustrated page 112

Tajima's abstracted images, solid structure, glowing colour, consistency and sheer imaginative power have made him one of the most popular artists of his day both in Japan and in the West. His technique consists of complicated superimpositions of woodblock, lighter colours over dark, the result always being a sense of incandescent light shining from behind the colour. His titles are allusive, often literary, and they are carefully chosen to guide the viewer's imagination in the right direction. In this example the 'dilapidation' could apply equally to blocks of masonry or to the strokes of the written characters of the Japanese language.

105 Hiroyuki Tajima

Poem of Deserted House
1975. 2nd of an edition of 50
Woodblock, 636 × 498mm
1981.2.26.03. Illustrated page 115

In this mainly red print Tajima again leads us by his title into speculation and ambiguity. The random black marks at the centre resemble scratches in a plaster wall, while the grille-shaped oblong towards the top has a brilliantly azure blue shining through it, like daylight. The three objects at the bottom resemble the stone pillar-foundations of a traditionally built Japanese house.

106 Sadao Watanabe 1913–

Feet washing
1972. 28th of an edition of 70
Stencil, 550 × 460mm
1978.10.9.05. Illustrated pages 28, 143

This print should not be confused with the rather similar *Washing the feet* of 1982, where Christ is standing over the disciple. Watanabe prints over Japanese hand-crumpled paper, often used to cover traditional book-wrappers or as end-papers for modern books, to give a feeling of rough, folk-like simplicity. Over this he stencils simple forms which, though Christian in subject, are reminiscent of the early Buddhist prints of Japan, most notably in the large, simplified eyes. Here the paper is dyed a mustard-yellow, with all the colours, including white, applied over it.

107 Iwao Akiyama 1921–

Falling Snow
1979. 8th of an edition of 100
Woodblock, 450 × 325mm
1980.1.28.033. Illustrated page 118

Akiyama has cultivated a deliberately rough technique of rather puddled black ink on hand-made paper with untrimmed edges and flecked with brown fragments of the outer bark of the paper mulberry. The effect is somewhat like the folk prints of earlier centuries. Yet this scene of a pilgrim climbing the snowy slopes of Mount Fuji is also in the more sophisticated tradition of *haiga* – sketches made to accompany the short verses called *haiku*. The inscription reads 'Fire on the mountain top; in the midst of life and death the snow keeps falling'.

124

125

126

subjects are often of country life which has changed little in the more remote parts of Japan. His point of view high above the foreground and almost non-existent horizon are also ancient Japanese compositional techniques. The subject is a village in the central mountains with cherry blossoms flowering in the late winter snows.

110 Yoshiharu Kimura 1934–

Gala Dress
1981. 10th of an edition of 75
Woodblock, 555 · 720mm
1982.3.1.03. Illustrated page 121

Kimura is not found in most books on contemporary Japanese prints, for he represents that side of native taste which is most different from the rest of the world's. It is a style of formalised patterning, seen at its forceful best in the *Rimpa* paintings of the seventeenth and eighteenth centuries, but at its worst whimsical. This composition is an opportunity for the artist to show off his immaculate technique in woodblock. The colours of the tail of the peacock are printed over a gilt and silvered surface which is itself impressed with a pattern like woven textile.

111 Fumiaki Fukita 1920–

Northern sea
1979. 5th of an edition of 50
Woodblock, 609 × 482mm
1980.12.29.06. Illustrated page 113

The title suggests the northern lights. Fukita's favourite theme is the night sky with stars, and he has developed a characteristic midnight blue to express his skies. In this print he is also recalling the startling firework displays traditional in Japan, especially the festival at the Ryōgoku Bridge in Tokyo which Horishige (1797–1858) depicted in a famous image from his series 'One hundred views of Edo'. Fukita, unlike the old master, uses woodblocks of different colours superimposed on each other to produce a kaleidoscopic effect of shifting tones and light.

112 Chimei Hamada 1917–

Eroding Town A
1977. 7th of an edition of 50
Engraving, aquatint, 310 × 230mm (image)
1982.7.30.01. Illustrated page 28

Hamada has rightly become one of the most internationally celebrated of contemporary print artists. Making no concessions to traditional technique, subject-matter or style, he has persistently produced his horrifying visions of nightmare, mental collapse, cruelty and desolation which seem to draw on the whole Western repertoire of artistic despair since Goya. This image marks a more recent trend in his work towards an art of blank

108 Fumio Kitaoka 1918–

Pond in Autumn, Moss Garden
1970. 92nd of an edition of 100
Woodblock, 560 × 402mm
1971.7.26.02. Illustrated page 109

The Japanese title is *Pond in Autumn at the Kokedera*. Kokedera means 'Moss Temple' and is the popular name for the celebrated Saihōji Temple on the western outskirts of Kyoto where the gardens consist of acres of dazzling moss punctuated by trees, ponds, rocks and houses for the Tea Ceremony. Kitaoka's simple shapes without outline are well suited to convey that nostalgia for the Japanese past

which is still strong both in Japan and among foreign visitors.

109 Mitsuhiro Unnō 1939–

Kinasa in light snow
1974. 9th of an edition of 100
Woodblock, 622 × 471mm
1981.7.29.01. Given by Dr Michael Rogers.
Illustrated page 29

Unnō, though relatively young, is one of the most traditionally minded of contemporary print artists. His simplified forms show the influence of Satō (see nos 92–3), while his

127

despair set in a soulless international cityscape. His people and even his dogs are literally without centres.

113 Naoko Matsubara 1937–

'Walden Pond'
The cover for the portfolio 'Solitude'
1971. 2nd of the 'preferred edition' of 25
Woodblock, 420 × 805 mm
(portfolio cover extended)
Published by Aquarius Press, Baltimore,
New York; printed by A. Colise,
Mount Vernon, New York, under the artist's
supervision
1980.10.24.01. Illustrated page 119

This portfolio includes eleven prints which illustrate the essay 'Solitude' from H.D. Thoreau's *Walden*. They are *Solitude*, *Pine*, *Wind*, *Winter Pond*, *Winter Serenity*, *Rain*, *Decaying Beauty*, *Autumn Colour*, *Spring Visitor*, *Thoreau* and *Drop of Life*. The print for the cover, in tones of green and white, is the most expansive and the boldest. It is also the most obviously Japanese in design by this artist, who has spent much of her working life in North America, notably in its brilliant patterning and its very high horizon.

114 Tetsuya Noda 1940–

Diary: March 3rd '77 (b)
Artist's proof
Mimeograph, woodblock, silk-screen,
598 × 842 mm
1982.11.09.03. Illustrated page 122

Noda has developed his own special technique which gives his prints their unique flavour. Taking his own photographs, with additions made by hand, he uses an electric scanning-machine to produce a vinyl stencil. With this he prints with ink through a silk-screen, using a large roller, on to a sheet of light buff-coloured Japanese paper. On to this he has already printed by the woodblock process any backgrounds he wishes to add, although these are normally very quiet in tone. The result looks from a distance or in reproduction very like a photograph. Its full subtlety and print-like flavour can be appreciated only by seeing the original, which will be surprisingly large.

Nearly all Noda's prints have since 1968 taken the form of a pictorial diary, beginning with the maturity of his new technique and inspired by his relationship with his future wife. In all of them he describes a moment both personal and universal, fixed in time and yet apparently timeless.

The artist's son, born in 1972, and daughter, born in 1974, have become the major subjects of his work since then. This print shows them together near a window in a room furnished in Western style. The sense of mystery which frequently prevails Noda's prints is abundantly expressed in this example.

133

129

115 Tetsuya Noda

Diary: August 10th '77
Artist's proof
Mimeograph, woodblock, silk-screen,
975 × 625mm
1982.11.09.07. Illustrated page 122

Wrapped up protectively in a *futon* (the Japanese quilt), the artist's daughter is caught in a moment of vulnerability, one of her slippers missing. She is standing on the polished wooden floors of the traditional-style corridor of a Japanese house, and the simple plaster wall is represented by white pigment printed by woodblock, contrasting with the pale buff paper.

116 Tetsuya Noda

Diary: March 31st '78
Artist's proof
Mimeograph, woodblock, silk-screen,
975 × 630mm
1982.11.09.010. Illustrated page 122

The artist's daughter, born in 1974, appears constantly in Noda's prints as she grows up, reflecting his and her feelings and development, and also the life of a Japanese child. Here she prepares to leave for her *Yōchien* (kindergarten), in uniform and heavily laden, except for the shoes which she will not put on until she leaves the house. Her 'Sketch Board' and satchel marked 'Candy Candy' in Japanese *katakana* script reflect the extreme prevalence of English in modern Japanese life.

117 Tetsuya Noda

Diary: August 2nd '79
Artist's proof
Mimeograph, woodblock, silk-screen,
975 × 632mm
1982.11.09.011. Illustrated page 123

This moment as the artist's daughter takes off her dress is extraordinarily touching. All of the vulnerability of a young child, and by implication of an adult, is expressed in this moment of uninhibited exposure. Noda has deliberately isolated her on a background printed dead-white in contrast to the buff tone of the paper which shows through the figure itself.

118 Tetsuya Noda

Diary: April 29th '80
Artist's proof
Mimeograph, woodblock, silk-screen,
973 × 626mm
1982.11.09.09. Illustrated page 123

The artist's daughter here disappears almost completely behind an old quilt (*futon*) leaving the viewer free to wonder what her mood was at that moment. Her unwillingness to be

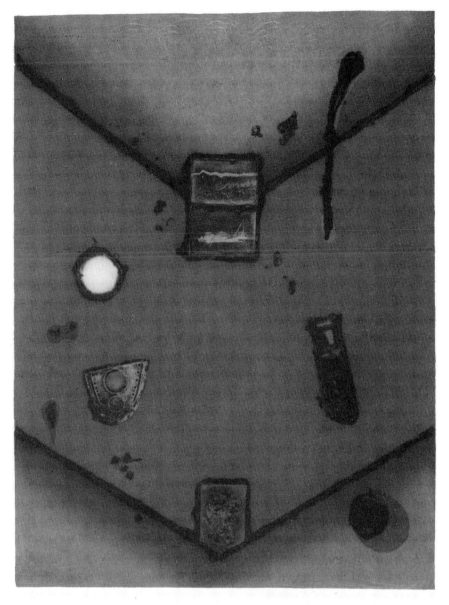

parted from the comforting quilt has provided the artist with many touching moments, which he contrives to make more universal by altering the photographic image into a print image.

119 Tetsuya Noda

Diary: June 25th '80
Artist's proof
Mimeograph, woodblock, silk-screen,
973 × 630mm
1982.11.09.08. Illustrated page 123

The faces of the artist's daughter and her kitten merge into each other, while the old quilt which she clings to tumbles over the edge of the print in rags which resemble rats' feet. It seems to be the very same blanket as in no. 118. Simple though this image appears,

it has a slightly sinister edge to it, suggesting that merging of a girl with an animal which is one of the persistent themes of Japanese myth.

134

120 Tetsuya Noda

Diary: July 22nd '80,
in Herezdira, Israel
Artist's proof
Mimeograph, woodblock, silk-screen,
600 × 832 mm
1982.11.09.06. Illustrated page 126

Noda's life has been greatly influenced by
Israel, for his wife, whom he married in
1971, is a native of that country. Just before
his marriage he announced his conversion to
Judaism. The meaning of this print, whatever
its personal impact for the artist, seems to be
the standardisation of life today. As a view of
a motorway it differs very little from no. 121,
a similar scene in Denmark. Yet in these very
samenesses Noda compels the viewer to see
subtle emotional differences by the very
intensity of his scrutiny.

121 Tetsuya Noda

Diary: August 10th '80,
in Helsingør, Denmark
Artist's proof
Mimeograph, woodblock, silk-screen,
592 × 835 mm
1982.11.09.04. Illustrated page 126

An extreme contrast between the man-made
world of a motorway and the natural world
of the stormy sky gives tension to this print.
The two are linked by the very tall lamp-post
seen from far below. The monotony of
modern technology is combined with the
distant hints of an older European civilisation
on the horizon.

122 Tetsuya Noda

Diary: September 6th '80,
in Darmstadt, Germany
Artist's proof
Mimeograph, woodblock, silk-screen,
594 × 837 mm
1982.11.09.02. Illustrated page 127

Noda's uncanny ability to take photographs
('sketches') which suggest both movement
and stillness at the same time is well
demonstrated here. A road intersection of
a busy city is shown as from inside an
approaching car. The whole scene seems
trapped under the web of electric car-cables.
Potential direction and actual direction seem
in conflict and produce a high tension.

123 Tetsuya Noda

Diary: June 12th '81. In Suidobashi
Artist's proof
Mimeograph, woodblock and silk-screen,
597 × 835mm
1982.11.09.05. Illustrated page 127

The name of the station, blurred almost
beyond recognition through the train window,
is Okikubo. One of the basic secrets of Noda's
success is his ability to choose the exact
moment to press the shutter of his camera.
Here we rush through a typically dreary
Tokyo suburban station, but the artist
compels the viewer to look at it anew. In
particular, the mysteriously blurred figure on
the platform concentrates attention on itself,
seen perhaps for the only time in the artist's
life and yet becoming part of it.

124 Osamu Morozumi 1949–

No. 18
1973. 33rd of an edition of 50
Woodblock, 978 × 636mm
1981.4.11.06. Illustrated page 130

Morozumi is unique in contemporary Japan
in using a stipple technique on wood. The
process of expressing volume by numerous
dots was at its height in Europe in the
eighteenth century, but it was carried out by
the intaglio method. Morozumi has adapted it
to the woodblock medium, using in each case
one very large, smoothed-off block into which
he cuts thousands of dots and shapes of
different sizes which show as white in reserve
from the surface, which is loaded with
lustrous black ink. With these means he
creates disturbing, untitled cauldrons of
three-dimensional movement, suggestive of
twisted viscera or dissolving sculptural forms.

125 Osamu Morozumi

No. 70
1977. 17th of an edition of 60
Woodblock, 879 × 637mm
1981.4.11.07. Illustrated page 131

Morozumi's prints are exceptionally three-
dimensional in effect owing to his emphasis
on *chiaroscuro*, which is not a Japanese
tradition. As a result, his designs are often
reminiscent of twentieth-century stone
sculpture. This perhaps explains the large
size of his prints, which need to be expansive
to contain the almost physical masses of his
forms.

135

136

126 Shigeyuki Kawachi 1948–

Pile

1980. 1st of an edition of 80
Woodblock, 964 × 668mm
1981.4.11.03. Illustrated page 132

Kawachi has been active since the early 1970s, when he already showed his very distinct obsession with depicting structures created by human beings in the modern world and therefore indirectly expressing some of the emotions and difficulties of that world. In this powerful vision, based on black, white and red, he shows a crane-load of boxes with the international marks used on the packing of fragile and delicate objects. They are destined for Venus, the planet of love, but the aspirations are too great and the whole structure is collapsing.

127 Shigeyuki Kawachi

Crack (1)

1980. 21st of an edition of 80
Woodblock, 668 × 958mm
1981.4.11.02. Illustrated page 133

Wood and its structures are among Kawachi's most persistent themes. As if to emphasise this he does small editions to bring out with the maximum clarity possible in this medium the very obtrusive grain of the large plywood blocks he uses, applying the colours to accentuate them where he wishes. Like many of his works, this example expresses the strain of contemporary life, which so often leads to breaking-point. To encompass these weighty visions he produces prints which are consistently among the biggest coming from Japan today.

128 Tokio Miyashita 1930–

Autumn Evening

c.1975. 29th of an edition of 50
Woodblock, intaglio, 700 × 510mm
1982.6.24.05. Illustrated page 116

Miyashita has developed an effective combination of metal intaglio with traditional woodblock on high-quality Japanese paper made by himself. The backgrounds are normally printed by woodblock in one brilliant colour – red, turquoise, green, tawny yellow – or shades of that colour. On it are scattered both abstract motifs and representations of real objects or people photographically transferred to metal plates which gouge deep into the background. Sometimes impressions of actual objects are used. The result is a surprisingly energetic mixture of abstraction, surrealism and Pop Art, often recalling in its pictorial structure the work of Miró. This 'nocturne' is predominantly a deep, glowing turquoise.

129 Tokio Miyashita

Work V-8

c.1975. 26th of an edition of 35
Woodblock, intaglio, 690 × 510mm
1982.6.24.06. Illustrated page 134

The small intaglio elements in black, yellow, white and grey float on the scorching red surface like dross on molten metal. At the top is a metal bracket used almost unmodified as a block, and at the top left a fragment of a calendar for January 195 . . . Down the right side runs a lurid black gash, almost like a reversed image of a wound.

130 Tokio Miyashita

Green and water

c.1975. 13th of an edition of 50
Woodblock, intaglio, 570 × 436mm
1983.3.11.01. Illustrated page 135

More recently Miyashita has increasingly included in his prints large human figures, usually female, taken from photographic images. The influence of Pop Art is very apparent in them. His earlier classic semi-abstract style as seen here, however, expresses his talent for sheer design better. This print is dominated by a broad, angled green band; at the top of it are two small yellow oblongs, one of a harbour and one of waves, which are taken from photographic images.

131 Ay-Ō 1931–

Pat-tap

c.1978. 65th of an edition of 350
Silk-screen, 325 × 495mm
Published at the Gendai Hanga Center, Tokyo
1981.2.27.02. Illustrated page 120

The artist's name, although it appears rather un-Japanese, is in fact written with two complex characters meaning 'cloud trailing nausea'. This jokiness conceals a superb and inventive technician, whose prints invariably used the colours of the rainbow in dazzling juxtapositions. He developed this technique in the late 1960s when he lived and worked in the USA for a number of years and participated in the Pop Art movement. The print is inscribed in Japanese 'This work can be seen vertically or horizontally'.

132 Kazumasa Nagai 1929–

Reverberation

1973. 260th of an edition of 300
Silk-screen, 656 × 483mm
1981.10.13.01. Illustrated page 117

The artist is best known for his all-white prints done in relief patterns with zinc blocks, but in this example he has produced a similar clean and rather severe effect with brilliant colour applied through a silk-screen, except for the white which is the paper's natural colour left untouched. Nagai's works are very much suited to modern décor in both private houses and office buildings, and are intended to hang on a wall, in direct contrast to the older Japanese tradition of having no permanent pictures at all on display.

133 Kunihiro Amano 1929–

Waking Dream II
1977
Woodblock, 670 × 965mm
1981.5.19.01. Illustrated page 128

The artist heightens the dreamlike atmosphere by making it unclear where the print begins and ends. At the bottom he has printed indented lines which isolate a border area between the main image and its surrounding paper, across which runs a pale half-coloured section of the twisting main subject. Although there is nothing in the title to suggest it, the twists and folds of the striped band in green, red and black are similar to the way a woman's sash (*obi*) is depicted in older styles of Japanese art. A simple example can be seen in no. 28 by Goyō.

134 Tetsurō Sawada 1933–

Night Island

1981. 15th of an edition of 35
Silk-screen, 598 × 790mm
1982.6.24.03. Illustrated page 136

Sawada's silk-screens, ultra-polished, streamlined, horizontally slanted, seem symbolic of his life as a contemporary print designer on the international circuit. Such men spend many hours in aircraft, and it is not fanciful to see a connection there with his recurrent images of mountains and clouds seen from far and high. Those who see no Japanese background in his work, however, are mistaken. His finely calculated overlaps of ragged-edged bands of closely contrasting colours have an ancient lineage in the paper collages used for writing poetry in Japan in the Heian period (AD 794–1185).

A Figure on the Ground

135 Kōsuke Kimura 1936–

Nō Mask – Black

c.1980. 9th of an edition of 60
Etched copperplate, 640 × 460mm
1981.2.27.04. Illustrated page 137

Kimura has become very admired on the
international scene for his collages in photo-
intaglio of numerous images from modern
life. More recently, however, he has produced
simpler images in a variety of techniques, of
which his *Nō Mask* series is one of the most
effective. He has used a photograph of a
mask used in the classic Japanese *Nō* drama
by actors playing parts of young women,
but by retaining the negative image has
surprisingly turned serenity into sinister
ferocity. This simple but very powerful print
has been achieved by etching a copperplate
through a half-tone screen, and then printing
in ink, the darkest parts being done by
mezzotint.

136 Katsurō Yoshida 1943–

Work 47 (Expectations)

1976. 40th of an edition of 75
Etching, 565 × 400mm
1982.6.24.04. Illustrated page 137

Yoshida has developed a special method of
using his own photographs to transfer on to
etching plates. He extracts from the
photograph, which he prints in a modified,
slightly blurred form, certain images which
seem the most significant to him. These he
prints above or below in isolation, with even
more altered surfaces. Thus he proceeds from
the general scene, closer to objective reality,
to his own personal, subjective feelings. In
this print the girl in the brutalised downtown
area of a Japanese city has detached herself
into a romantic, human vision. Yoshida uses
French paper for this intaglio process.

137 Shin Kamiya 1942–

Rock Rock Fire

c.1980. 56th of an edition of 150
Silk-screen, 610 × 865mm
1981.10.13.02. Illustrated page 124

Kamiya is a most striking example of that
unity of the old and the new which
characterises so many young Japanese artists.
Using a photographically produced stencil for
the silk-screen technique, he aims to
reproduce the complexities of traditional ink
painting. Shinoda did it before him with
lithograph, but he has taken a further
imaginative jump by translating black ink
into colour. His original photographs are
much altered at the negative stage to
produce shapes full of movement and
mystery.

138 Shigeki Kuroda 1953–

Run Away
c.1981. 39th of an edition of 50
Etching, aquatint, 680 × 575mm
1982.6.24.01. Illustrated page 139

Like many younger artists in Japan, Kuroda has taken to intaglio techniques and breathed new life into them. In his prints, which almost always show crowds of people with umbrellas, normally speeding by on bicycles, he uses etched copperplates with aquatint, drypoint, and other modifications. This example is in black and white, but he also uses colour, though perhaps to less effect. His very monothematic images give an intense feeling of the speed, crush and insensitivity of contemporary life, which are particularly noticeable in the great cities of Japan.

139 Toshiyuki Shiroki 1938–

Dissolve
1981. 1st of an edition of 30
Copperplate, mezzotint, 766 × 554mm
1982.7.26.02. Illustrated pages 1, 140

Like Kimura (no. 142), Shiroki uses a combination of copperplate etched through a screen taken from a photograph with a lustrous black background done by mezzotint. His intense contemplation of a melting steel girder applies a typically Japanese concentration to an industrial subject. Like other recent artists, he has begun to discover the possibilities of the old European techniques of etching and mezzotint to express his more native sensibility. There is a freshness about his approach to these intaglio techniques which was lost long ago in the West.

140 Yoichi Takahara 1944–

A Figure on the Ground
1981. 2nd of an edition of 8
Silk-screen, 800 × 1,185mm (image)
1982.7.26.01. Illustrated page 141

This print marks an even more extreme move towards size than the works of Takahashi, Kawachi and Morozumi, and it is difficult to see where such a work could find a home except on the walls of a major museum or gallery. So big is it that the artist has had to print through two separate silk-screens, joining vertically down the middle. Like many of his contemporaries, he has printed through a stencil prepared from a photographic film; the photograph itself is of one of the artist's own constructions. In that sense it is the ultimate development so far of the 'creative print'.

141 Mokuden Fujimoto 1895–

'Studies of bamboo'
From *A Picture Album of the Four Noble Plants*
1973. From a limited edition of 20
Photographic reproduction, 252 × 335mm (each page)
Published by the Mokuden Society, printed by the Akatsuki Printing Company, Tokuyama
1976.11.1.06. Presented by the artist.
Illustrated page 30

This book is one of three which celebrated the *Nanga* (Chinese-style painting) of Mokuden, latest in a line of artists beginning with Chikuden (1775–1835). The 'four noble plants' beloved of Chinese artists and scholars are epidendrum, bamboo, chrysanthemum and plum. The book, on a very thin 'Chinese' paper allows the subject on the previous page to show through. In this illustration the bamboo on the left is in orange, while that on the right (reversed from the previous page) is green.

142 Rokurō Mutō 1907–

'The Paper Mulberry and the Mitsumata Plant'
From the book *Tie-dyeing and woodblock*
1978. 39th of a limited edition of 280
Woodblock, 285 × 200mm (each page)
Published by Ibunkaku, Kyoto
1979.10.15.01. Illustrated page 30

This very traditionally produced book, as befits a famous craftsman of the Folk Art movement, includes original examples of the dyed papers by Mutō, as well as his decorative woodblock prints of the zodiac animals and of aspects of paper-making. The prints and papers were entirely produced by the artist. The subject illustrated is printed in green on paper flecked with mulberry bark.

143 Tsunemitsu Konishi 1940–

'Rainwater basin' (left) and 'Mountain entrance of the Jōjakkōji'
From the book *One Hundred Views of Sagano*, Kyoto
1975. 61st of an edition of 100
Photographic reproduction from pen and ink drawing, 240 × 255mm (each page)
Published by Fujioka Kentarō at the Kyoto Shoin; plates made by the New Colour Printing Company
1979.10.15.03. Illustrated page 30

This book is the modern equivalent of the old *ehon* (picture-books) of favourite sets of views which had flourished in the early nineteenth century. It shows the picturesque old area of Kyoto called Sagano near to the western mountains, with a nostalgic text by Yoshiro Takaguma.

106. Sadao Watanabe (1913–). *Feet washing*, 1972. Stencil

Bibliography

The books in English on Japanese prints of this century are few and uneven. For many subjects the only accurate information is in art journals or exhibition catalogues, which are not quoted here since they are difficult for the ordinary reader to acquire. One Japanese publication must be mentioned, however, since it is much the finest collection of reproductions available and has short English captions – *Kindai Nihon Hanga Taikei* ('A Survey of Recent Japanese Prints'), published by Mainichi Newspapers, Tokyo, 1975, in three volumes.

The following is a short list of easily available books with useful information:

FRANCES BLAKEMORE
Who's Who in Modern Japanese Prints,
New York and Tokyo, 1975

JAMES MICHENER
The Floating World,
London, 1955

JAMES MICHENER
The Modern Japanese Print: An Appreciation,
Rutland, Vermont and Tokyo, 1968
(a small-scale reproduction version of the book described in no. 91a)

OLIVER STATLER
Modern Japanese Prints: An Art Reborn,
Rutland, Vermont and Tokyo, 1959, 1980

TOMIKICHIRŌ TOKURIKI
Woodblock Printing,
Tokyo, 1966, 1977

Index of artists